Universal Database Management

A Guide to Object/Relational Technology

The Morgan Kaufmann Series in Data Management Systems

Series Editor, Jim Gray

A Complete Guide to DB2 Universal Database
Don Chamberlin

Universal Database Management: A Guide to Object/Relational Technology
Cynthia Maro Saracco

Understanding SQL's Stored Procedures: A Complete Guide to SQL/PSM
Jim Melton

Principles of Multimedia Database Systems
V. S. Subrahmanian

Principles of Database Query Processing for Advanced Applications
Clement T. Yu and Weiyi Meng

The Object Database Standard: ODMG 2.0
R. G. G. Cattell et al.

Introduction to Advanced Database Systems
Carlo Zaniolo, Stefano Ceri, Christos Faloutsos, Richard Snodgrass, V. S. Subrahmanian, and Roberto Zicari

Principles of Transaction Processing
Philip A. Bernstein and Eric Newcomer

Using the New DB2: IBM's Object-Relational Database System
Don Chamberlin

Distributed Algorithms
Nancy A. Lynch

Object-Relational DBMSs: The Next Great Wave
Michael Stonebraker with Dorothy Moore

Active Database Systems: Triggers and Rules For Advanced Database Processing
Edited by Jennifer Widom and Stefano Ceri

Joe Celko's SQL for Smarties: Advanced SQL Programming
Joe Celko

Migrating Legacy Systems: Gateways, Interfaces, and the Incremental Approach
Michael L. Brodie and Michael Stonebraker

Database: Principles, Programming, and Performance
Patrick O'Neil

Database Modeling and Design: The Fundamental Principles, Second Edition
Toby J. Teorey

Readings in Database Systems, Second Edition
Edited by Michael Stonebraker

Atomic Transactions
Nancy Lynch, Michael Merritt, William Weihl, and Alan Fekete

Query Processing for Advanced Database Systems
Edited by Johann Christoph Freytag, David Maier, and Gottfried Vossen

Transaction Processing: Concepts and Techniques
Jim Gray and Andreas Reuter

Understanding the New SQL: A Complete Guide
Jim Melton and Alan R. Simon

Building an Object-Oriented Database System: The Story of O_2
Edited by François Bancilhon, Claude Delobel, and Paris Kanellakis

Database Transaction Models for Advanced Applications
Edited by Ahmed K. Elmagarmid

A Guide to Developing Client/Server SQL Applications
Setrag Khoshafian, Arvola Chan, Anna Wong, and Harry K. T. Wong

The Benchmark Handbook for Database and Transaction Processing Systems, Second Edition
Edited by Jim Gray

Camelot and Avalon: A Distributed Transaction Facility
Edited by Jeffrey L. Eppinger, Lily B. Mummert, and Alfred Z. Spector

Readings in Object-Oriented Database Systems
Edited by Stanley B. Zdonik and David Maier

Universal Database Management

A Guide to Object/Relational Technology

Cynthia Maro Saracco

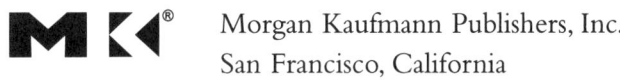
Morgan Kaufmann Publishers, Inc.
San Francisco, California

Senior Editor	Diane Cerra	Copyeditor	Ken DellaPenta
Director of Production and Manufacturing	Yonie Overton	Proofreader	Jennifer McClain
		Compositor	Technologies 'N Typography
Production Editor	Elisabeth Beller	Illustrator	Cherie Plumlee
Cover Design	Ross Carron Design	Indexer	Ted Laux
Cover Image	Imtek Imagineering/Masterfile	Printer	Courier Corporation
Text Design	Ross Carron Design		

Designations used by companies to distinguish their products are often claimed as trademarks or registered trademarks. In all instances where Morgan Kaufmann Publishers, Inc. is aware of a claim, the product names appear in initial capital or all capital letters. Readers, however, should contact the appropriate companies for more complete information regarding trademarks and registration.

Morgan Kaufmann Publishers, Inc.
Editorial and Sales Office
340 Pine Street, Sixth Floor
San Francisco, CA 94104-3205
USA
Telephone   415/392-2665
Facsimile   415/982-2665
Email   mkp@mkp.com
WWW   http://www.mkp.com

Order toll free 800/745-7323

© 1998 Morgan Kaufmann Publishers, Inc.
All rights reserved
Printed in the United States of America

02   01   00   99   98   5   4   3   2   1

No part of this publication may be reproduced, stored in a retrieval system, or transmitted in any form or by any means—electronic, mechanical, photocopying, recording, or otherwise—without the prior written permission of the publisher.

Library of Congress Cataloging-in-Publication Data

Saracco, Cynthia Maro
    Universal database management : a guide to object/relational technology / Cynthia Maro Saracco.
      p.   cm.
    Includes bibliographical references and index.
    ISBN 1-55860-519-3
    1. Database managment. 2. Object-oriented databases.
3. Relational databases. I. Title.
QA76.9.D3S2545   1998
005.74—dc21   96-20254
                                                                                                                                    CIP

In memory of Herschel K. Saracco, who passed away during the development of this book

Foreword

Jim Gray

This is an excellent introduction to *universal databases,* also known as *object/relational databases.* Universal databases extend the traditional relational database model to include the object-oriented benefits of encapsulation, polymorphism, and inheritance. They integrate the best features of passive relational databases, active databases (assertions, stored procedures, and triggers), and object-oriented programming (abstract data types, classes, methods, and inheritance). The resulting systems are better able to manage the rich data types of the Internet. The ideas are especially useful in managing multimedia, spatial, and temporal data. Universal databases allow a new business model in which application developers can buy components (also called blades, cartridges, or extenders) in a commodity marketplace. This component-based programming model is a productivity breakthrough for application developers. There has been intense research and experimentation on universal databases over the last decade. The dust is now settling. A consensus is emerging in the SQL3 standard. All the major database vendors have announced their "universal" products reflecting this consensus.

This book is written in light of this consensus on the core concepts and basic approach to universal databases. The book is a quick read made even quicker by the margin notes that outline each page. The text walks you through basic object-oriented concepts, then shows how they dovetail with relational and active database concepts. It talks about competing ideas and technologies and gives a balanced analysis of the pros and cons of each. The writing is pragmatic, going from concept to instance with many examples drawn from IBM's DB2 Universal Database. The book ends with an excellent glossary and references.

There is little question that these ideas are the basis for the next generation of database systems. This book is a great place to start learning about these ideas. Cynthia Maro Saracco brings her years of experience as an application designer, a consultant, and a teacher to this book. It is a compact, modern, and accessible introduction that, in a few hours, teaches you the basic concepts and terminology of universal databases.

Contents

Foreword	**vii**
Preface	**xv**

CHAPTER 1
Coping with Complexity — 1

Evolution of Data Management	1
An Industry at the Crossroads	4
Object-Oriented Programming	5
"Specialized" Data vs. Corporate Data	10
The World Wide Web	13
Which Way to Turn?	15
The Revolutionary Approach	15
The Evolutionary Approach	16
Universal Database Management Systems Arrive	18
Summary	19

CHAPTER 2
Merging Object and Relational Technologies — 21

Moving Beyond Simple Character Strings and Numbers	22
Creating New Data Types	23
Business Value	24
Recognizing Business Rules	25
Triggers	25
Stored Procedures	27

User-Defined Functions	28
Business Value	29
Supporting Flexible Table Structures	30
Rows with Multivalue Columns	30
Complex Data Types	31
Business Value	32
Ensuring High Performance	33
Custom Index Structures for New Data Types	34
Enhanced Optimization	34
Indexes for Functions	35
Business Value	35
Leveraging Ready-Made Class Libraries	36
Business Value	36
Summary	37

CHAPTER 3
Managing New, Simple Data Types — 39

Supporting Large Objects	40
Storing Large Objects	41
Working with Large Objects	41
Tuning for Performance	43
Reducing Log Activities	45
Creating New Types of Simple Data	47
Simple Types	48
Integrity Implications	50
Type Casting	51
Summary	53

CHAPTER 4
Working with Complex Data — 55

What Is "Complex" Data?	55
Using Complex Types for Column Definitions	56

Example	58
Working with Columns That Contain Structured Data	60
Advanced Issues	65
Using Complex Types to Define Table Structures	65
Example	66
Creating References to Complex Types	68
Using References to Access Data	71
Referential Integrity vs. References	72
Summary	74

CHAPTER 5
Building Business Knowledge into the DBMS — 77

Enforcing Business Rules Automatically	78
Constraints	79
Triggers	80
Linking DBMS Events to External Events	88
Customizing SQL to Meet Your Needs	90
Example	91
Simple vs. Complex Functions	92
Performance, Security, and Administrative Issues	93
Synergy with User-Defined Types and Large Objects	94
Function Overloading	97
Encouraging Code Reuse	98
Benefits of Stored Procedures	99
Writing Stored Procedures	101
Summary	102

CHAPTER 6
Modeling Data in New Ways — 105

Refining and Extending Data Types	106
Subtyping a Complex Type	107
Substituting One Type for Another	110

Creating Type "Blueprints"	111
Type Hierarchies and Table Definitions	112
Managing Table Hierarchies	114
Table Hierarchy Example	115
Working with Table Hierarchies	116
Storing Table Hierarchies	118
Using Collections	119
Defining Tables with Multivalue Columns	120
Building Nested Table Structures	124
Combining Complex Types, Collections, and Hierarchies	126
Managing Type Creation	128
Summary	129

CHAPTER 7
Providing Quick Access to Custom Data — 133

Indexing	134
Index Structure in a Relational DBMS	134
New Index Structures for New Data Types	137
Maintaining External Indexes	138
Extending Existing Index Structures	142
Introducing Completely New Index Structures	145
Indexing User-Defined Functions	147
Optimization	149
Providing Optimization Hints or Instructions	151
Influencing Cost Estimation	153
Summary	155

CHAPTER 8
Using Class Libraries — 157

What Are Class Libraries?	157
Spatial Data Library	160
Time Series Data Library	163

Text Data Library	166
Image Data Library	168
Video Data Library	170
Other Class Libraries	171
Class Libraries and Industry Standards	172
Summary	173

CHAPTER 9
Distributed Data, Universally Managed — 175

File Links for Managing External Data	175
Business Value	176
Typical Capabilities	178
Sample Architecture	182
Multidatabase Servers	183
Business Value	185
Typical Capabilities	187
Sample Architecture	192
Summary	197

CHAPTER 10
Alternatives to Universal DBMSs — 199

Overview	199
Object DBMSs	201
Object/Relational Mapping Services	205
Specialized Servers with an Integration Layer	208
Component-Based Software	211
Summary	213

CHAPTER 11
What's the Bottom Line? — 217

Business Benefits	217
Common Criticisms	219

Future Trends 221
Summary 223

CHAPTER 12
Is Universal Database Management Right for You? 225

Evaluation Guidelines 225
    Types of Data to Be Managed 226
    Business Rules to Be Enforced 227
    Performance Issues 229
    Complementary Tools and Class Libraries 230
    Standards Compliance and "Openness" 231
    Integration with Existing IT Systems 232
    Other Issues 233
Issues to Consider Before Deployment 233
    Staffing Issues 234
    IT Environmental Issues 234
    Target Applications 235
Summary 237

Glossary 239
References and Related Readings 249
Index 257

Preface

Increased business pressures and a changing Information Technology (IT) landscape have left firms demanding more from their database management systems (DBMSs) than these systems were originally designed to support. During the last several years, most major DBMS vendors have invested heavily in object/relational technology to provide the extensibility and flexibility that many organizations now require. These investments have spawned the development of "universal" DBMSs. Such products—although by no means homogeneous—generally seek to

- manage diverse data types in an integrated fashion
- offer greater support for object-oriented programming languages (such as C++ and Java)
- provide for greater synergy with World Wide Web applications
- help firms analyze many forms of critical business data in new ways to gain a competitive advantage

Although universal DBMSs seem poised to have a significant impact on the IT industry, few efforts have been made to describe the technology in a simple and straightforward manner, explore its business value in clear terms, and offer guidelines to determine when universal DBMSs might be most useful and how to successfully prepare for deployment. This book attempts to fill that gap, providing IT professionals with a "quick read" on this important new technology.

If you're not already familiar with object-oriented concepts, relational DBMS technology, or the Structured Query Language (SQL), don't worry. This book explains the essentials in plain, simple terms. As much as possible, examples are drawn from the emerging International Organization for Standardization (ISO) "SQL3" specification to provide a reasonably vendor-independent discussion of universal DBMS technology. Note that this specification was not in its final form as of this writing, although many areas were considered to be "stable." At any rate, concepts, not SQL syntax, are the focus of this exploration.

Occasionally, this book uses vendor-specific examples to illustrate key functions that are typically outside the scope of the SQL standards body. Given my professional background, such examples often draw from IBM technology, although you'll also find discussions of technologies specific to Oracle, Informix, Microsoft, and others.

Finally, this book is best approached as a starting point for understanding universal DBMSs and object/relational technology. It discusses all major technical areas, but doesn't aim to do so in an exhaustive manner or discuss every vendor-specific implementation. Rather, this book concentrates on the essentials of the technology and the business value that the technology can bring to many IT organizations.

Acknowledgments

Thanks are due to the many people who reviewed one or more drafts of this book, provided important reference material, or otherwise helped with the publication of the manuscript. In alphabetical order, those who contributed their technical expertise include Don Chamberlin, Dan Clarke, Stefan Dessloch, Orv Einsiedel, Don Haderle, Kathy Komer, Nelson Mattos, Prem Mehra, Inderpal Narang, Steve Roti, Yun Wang, and Karen Watterson. In addition, the staff at Morgan Kaufmann—particularly Diane Cerra, Elisabeth Beller, and Antonia Richmond—did an outstanding job throughout the editorial and production stages. And finally, special thanks are due to David Saracco for his assistance with the cover design and patience throughout the development of this text.

Any opinions expressed in this book, as well as any errors or omissions, are strictly my own.

CHAPTER 1

Coping with Complexity

For more than three decades, firms have used various file systems and database management systems (DBMSs) to manage one of their most critical corporate assets: their data. The data stored in these systems typically consists of simple types—such as character strings and numbers—that contain customer names, invoice numbers, departmental budgets, suppliers' addresses, and the like. While the need to manage such data isn't likely to change, many companies now find themselves needing more from their DBMSs in order to cope with an increasingly complex business environment.

Data remains a key corporate asset.

Evolution of Data Management

In the early days of computing, simple business data was stored in operating system files. Programmers tailored the format of data records within these files to meet the needs of their particular applications. As more and more applications were built, critical business data was spread across more and more files. This created at least two significant problems:

File systems aren't enough.

- Working with data in multiple files required considerable knowledge of the contents and structure of each file. Furthermore, security issues were often a concern.
- Some data was duplicated in multiple files, making maintenance difficult. For example, employee names might appear in files associated with payroll processing, work schedules, performance appraisals, project management, and facilities maintenance. If an employee's name changed, it would have to be reflected in many files. Identifying all affected files and making the necessary changes in each was often difficult and cumbersome.

DBMSs manage shared data efficiently.

These problems, and others, helped create the need for DBMS products that made it easier and more practical to share data among various applications. Over time, sophisticated support for recovering from failures, managing concurrent access to data, maintaining high levels of availability, preserving the integrity of data, and performing other useful functions were built into DBMSs.

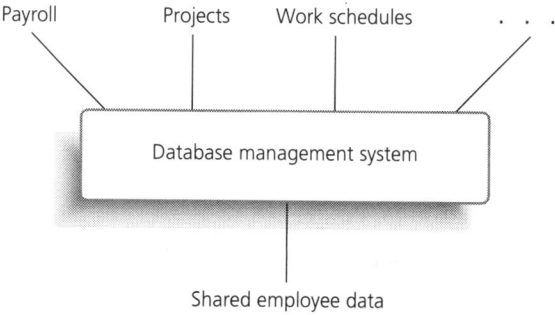

Early DBMSs required substantial programming.

In the 1970s through early 1980s, two types of DBMSs were particularly popular: hierarchic DBMSs and network (sometimes called "CODASYL") DBMSs. These systems—run largely on mainframe computers—structured data in specific ways. Hierarchic DBMSs, such as IBM's Information Management System (IMS), stored data in treelike hierarchies. Network DBMSs, such as the Integrated

Database Management System (IDMS) developed by Cullinet and later acquired by Computer Associates, stored data in a more complex two-level tree structure. Both types of DBMSs required programmers to *navigate* through these structures by following visible links between related data elements. Doing so often required considerable programming skill. Although many of these systems are still in use today, they no longer represent the majority of the DBMS market.

By the early to mid-1980s, a number of products emerged based on a different data model—the relational data model. Relational DBMSs differed significantly from prerelational DBMSs in several ways. These systems used a simple table-based structure and a query interface that enabled users to specify *what* data they wanted without having to instruct the DBMS on *how* to get to it. Relational DBMSs soon became the technology of choice for managing departmental and corporate data.

Relational DBMSs were a breakthrough.

ID	NAME	DEPT	JOB	SALARY
12-456	J. Smith	D12	Manager	85,000
08-652	D. Wilson	J15	Sales Rep	40,000
97-877	F. Drake	L80	Accountant	65,000

Data is stored in simple tables.

The lack of visible links between data elements and a new value-based interface helped prevent applications from "breaking" when some element of the underlying database structure needed to be changed to accommodate new business requirements. This contributed to *data independence*. The set-oriented nature of relational DBMSs—operations could be performed on multiple rows of a table rather than just individual data records—helped improve programmer productivity. The introduction and adoption of a new

Access is easier and doesn't require navigation.

database language (the Structured Query Language, or SQL) brought a greater level of consistency across DBMS products. A high-level database access language, SQL offered the potential to enable non-programmers to write ad hoc queries and generate reports in real time. And because the relational data model itself was based on set theory and modern logic, it offered a level of formality and precision frequently lacking in other approaches.

Relational DBMSs are now widely used.

Relational DBMSs now constitute a multibillion dollar industry and are widely deployed in firms throughout the world. Since the 1980s, they have been available for many platforms, ranging from mainframes to small workstations and personal computers. Leading software vendors, such as IBM, Informix, Microsoft, Oracle, and Sybase, derive significant revenue from such products and consider them an integral part of their business strategies. Similarly, vendors of popular tools and applications—such as SAP, Computer Associates, Platinum, and others—have also based offerings around relational DBMSs.

An Industry at the Crossroads

But they're not without limitations.

Yet despite their commercial success, relational DBMS products are occasionally criticized as being inflexible and slow to adapt to broader changes in the computing landscape. With Information Technology (IT) playing a greater role in the ultimate success of many businesses, market pressures have forced IT vendors to become increasingly innovative, seeking ways to turn private and academic research efforts into offerings that can help firms gain a competitive edge. This has created a vastly more complex IT environment than was present in most organizations a mere decade ago.

New business and technical pressures pose challenges for relational DBMSs.

Among the changes posing problems for traditional relational DBMSs are

- the popularity of object-oriented programming languages, such as C++, Java, and Smalltalk

- the desire to store, manage, and integrate "unusual" or nontraditional data with the more conventional numeric and alphanumeric business data stored in relational DBMSs
- the growth of the World Wide Web, which in turn spawned many commercial Internet, intranet, and extranet activities

To understand how each poses a problem for traditional relational DBMSs, let's take a closer look.

Object-Oriented Programming

Object-oriented (OO) programming languages began to capture the attention of IT organizations in the 1980s and are now the development paradigm of choice in many organizations. Why? Quite simply, certain characteristics of these languages promise to bring additional value to businesses.

Object-oriented technology emerges.

Code reuse is one potential benefit. A given firm may have millions of dollars invested in applications, some of which contain modules that perform very similar (if not exactly the same) functions found in other modules or applications. This hardly leverages the full potential of the application programming staff. Furthermore, it presents a maintenance headache. Facilities built into object-oriented programming languages help encourage code reuse, as we'll see later.

Firms hope to be able to reuse code and reduce maintenance costs.

In addition, object-oriented programming languages provide a flexibility not found in more traditional languages. Among other things, this flexibility helps programmers model their applications in a manner more comprehensible to the business staff destined to use the applications. Miscommunication between IT staff and business staff frequently contributes to a poor understanding of application requirements. The resulting application often misses the mark, much to the frustration of all involved. Object-oriented analysis and design techniques help bridge this communication gap, potentially enabling

OO languages are quite flexible.

programmers to translate user requirements into working code more effectively.

Those are just two of the potential benefits of object-oriented programming languages that have contributed to their increased popularity. What mechanisms do they employ to achieve this?

New types of objects can be defined.

Object-oriented programming languages—including C++, Java, and Smalltalk—differ from traditional, procedural languages in many ways. First, data and the code that operates on it are not treated separately in object-oriented programming languages. Instead, programmers work with *objects*—entities thought to consist of both data and code. Furthermore, object-oriented programmers frequently define new *types* or *classes* of objects to help them more readily represent the real-world entities with which their applications work. These entities might be business documents, employees, customers, insurance policies, bank accounts—just about any type of entity important to the business. The very nature of object-oriented programming can prompt many developers to modularize their code, thereby promoting code reuse.

These objects consist of data and code.

What's unique about objects from a programming viewpoint is that they aren't just data. Defining a new type or class of object involves specifying its *attributes* (data characteristics) and its *methods* (valid functions or services). For example, an EMPLOYEE object may have attributes defined for the employee's name, salary, serial number, phone number, and so on. It may also have methods defined to transfer employees from one location to another, generate a performance appraisal report, alter a compensation package, and so on.

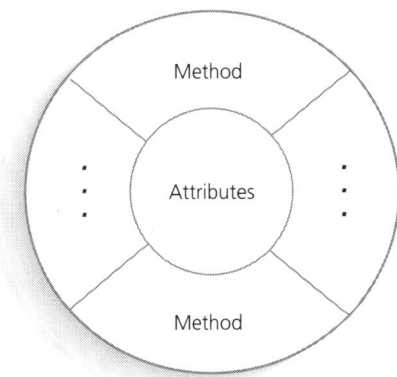

Data elements (values for attributes) are encapsulated by code (methods) that determine valid operations.

These methods *encapsulate* the underlying data. In other words, people don't work directly with the underlying data elements but instead invoke appropriate methods—or send *messages* to the object—to do so. Encapsulation helps insulate the application from any changes to the underlying data structure that was part of class definition. You see, class designers can use a variety of data structures for their objects—arrays, linked lists, tables (collections), and so on. There isn't one mandatory form. And these objects don't need to be based on just simple data types, such as character strings and numbers.

Object-oriented concepts introduce some problems for programmers who want to store their objects in relational DBMSs or to perceive data already stored in a relational DBMS as "objects." First, relational DBMS products were originally built to support only traditional types of data—character strings, varying-length character

Mapping object concepts to a relational world can be tough.

strings, decimals, integers, and so on. Each DBMS has its own set of supported data types. Thus, object-oriented programmers have to find a way to map their new types of objects to the specific set of data types supported by their DBMS. Since a single object definition may contain many different attributes—some of which themselves may be other objects—this type mapping is no trivial matter.

Differences in data types and data structures supported are just two reasons.

Second, relational DBMSs have traditionally made a clean delineation between data and code. Data exists and is managed independently, without "methods" or other user code to encapsulate it. Data access is accomplished by writing queries in SQL—a standard language supported by all major vendors. Early definitions of SQL did not include the notion of operators and functions that were defined by a programmer.

Third, relational DBMSs employ a tabular data structure. Users perceive their data as being stored in rows of a table. Object-oriented languages enable programmers to create new types of objects that employ any data structure that the programmer cares to build. Again, this poses a problem when trying to bridge between an "object" view of the world and a "relational" view of the world.

Class hierarchies and inheritance encourage code reuse.

But the problems don't stop there. Object-oriented programming languages introduce the concept of *class hierarchies.* Briefly, programmers can create new classes of objects that are subclasses of previously defined classes. This allows for incremental refinement, enabling programmers to leverage the work of others as they create new classes to meet their needs.

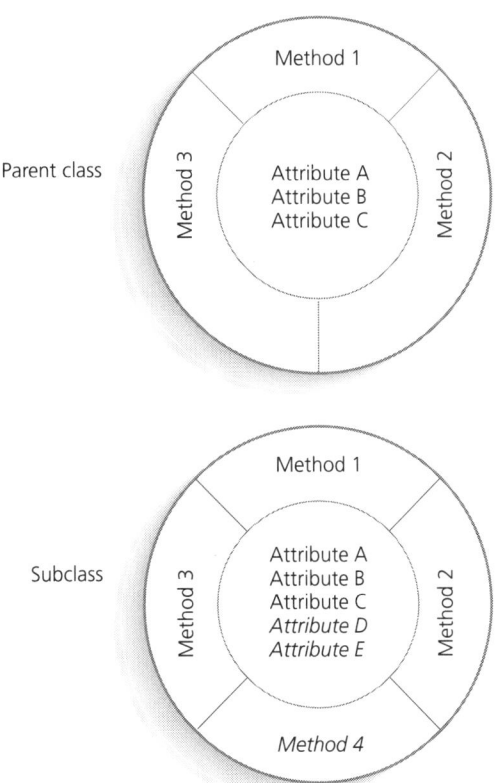

New classes can be derived from existing classes.

Because subclasses *inherit* the attributes and methods of their "parent" classes, coding requirements are minimized. Programmers only need to define the new attributes or methods that distinguish a subclass from its parent(s). The rest of the code is inherited "for free."

To see how this works, consider the earlier EMPLOYEE example. To better model employees, a firm might wish to define a subclass for EXECUTIVEs. While executives possess the same basic characteristics of all employees and may require the same set of services, they're also unique in some respects. Executives may be eligible for a quarterly bonus—a new attribute that must be considered. And this affects the

The attributes and methods of the parent class are automatically inherited by the subclass.

service—or method—that calculates their overall compensation. By defining `EXECUTIVE`s as a subclass of `EMPLOYEE`, a programmer merely needs to write the code for the new attribute and the revised compensation method.

Again, the notions of type (or class) hierarchies and inheritance were principles not originally incorporated into relational DBMS products. And again, lack of DBMS support for such notions helps contribute to the *impedance mismatch* between relational DBMSs and object-oriented applications.

But hierarchies and inheritance weren't part of early relational DBMSs.

This impedance mismatch occurs (in part) because the range of types and structures supported by an object-oriented programming language aren't supported in a traditional relational DBMS. Thus, programmers must try to map their objects into the data types and tabular structure supported by the DBMS. In practice, this can be difficult to do, often introducing semantic and performance issues.

There is more to this, of course. Object-oriented programming languages introduced a number of other concepts and techniques that we haven't discussed yet. But without going into all the details, the point is this: traditional relational DBMSs face some challenges to be able to effectively support object-oriented applications.

"Specialized" Data vs. Corporate Data

Support for image, full-text, and other types of data can also be a problem.

Another challenge facing DBMS vendors involves support for "specialized" or nontraditional forms of data. As we saw earlier, most DBMS products, including relational DBMSs, were originally designed to manage financial data, customer data, employee data, supplier data, and the like. This information could easily be represented with various forms of character strings and numbers.

But over the course of the past decade, it has become clear that important business data isn't just confined to these traditional forms. Images, full-text documents, geographic data (such as maps), and other types of data often play a key role in many industries. The challenge, then, involves effectively managing such nontraditional data and enabling users to write queries that involve both traditional and nontraditional types.

For example, a mail-order firm in the clothing industry might wish to maintain images of catalog items available for purchase. Of course, this same firm might like to associate more "mundane" business data with these images, such as order numbers, prices, fabric content data, supplier data, and so on. In addition, this firm might like to enable its employees—and perhaps its potential customers—to search through this electronic catalog in various ways. These search activities might be required to

- generate a report listing all the women's wool blazers that have a herringbone pattern and are priced at less than $200
- determine if any red silk ties with a paisley print are in stock
- list the manufacturer and model names of all women's dress shoes that have at least a 1-inch heel and match the color of dress #1245

Note that all such inquiries require analyzing both the content of the image and the content of the "traditional" business data in some way. Relational DBMSs weren't originally built to do that. And of course, images aren't the only form of specialized data that businesses have come to use. Some other forms of specialized data include the following:

Yet many firms need to analyze and manage both traditional and unusual types of data.

Multimedia, geographic, time series, and custom data types are all increasingly important.

- **Multimedia data.** Image, audio, video, and text documents are common forms. Of these, text is the most widely used. Employee appraisals, business reports, marketing brochures, and press releases are all examples of documents containing important business data. In certain industries, such as the entertainment and news industries, audio and video are of particular importance.

- **Geographic data.** A common form of spatial data, geographic data tracks information such as the location of customers' homes, the boundaries of a city, the location of utility lines (for water, gas, electricity), and so on. Often, such information is represented with points, lines, and polygons. Points identify a specific location in a broader region, such as the location of a store in New York City. Lines are useful for representing roads, highways, and railways. And polygons identify regions, such as a state boundary or an area occupied by a lake. Many industries rely on geographic data, including retail, insurance, petroleum/gas, transportation, government, and utilities.

- **Time series data.** Although most people think of time using the standard calendar of 365 days per year, other calendaring systems are essential in certain business contexts. For example, the number of workdays per year differs from the number of calendar days. This difference affects project management. Similarly, the number of valid stock-trading days per year is not 365. This affects various financial applications.

- **Custom data.** Many industries have their own forms of data peculiar to their work. For example, fingerprint data is essential to many law enforcement agencies. Specialized routines may need to be applied to fingerprint data that would not be conducive to analysis of more generic image data. Similarly, currency is a specialized form of numeric data. Account balances with different types of currency (such as US dollars and Japanese yen) should not be compared directly.

Being able to store these unusual data types isn't enough. New data types introduce new analytic needs. For example, geographic data introduces the need for geographic analysis, such as the ability to determine the relationship between two entities based on their relative location. A simple example might involve determining all the Italian restaurants within a 1-mile distance of a particular hotel. To resolve this inquiry, the system would need to support traditional forms of business analysis involving character string data (to determine which restaurants serve "Italian" cuisine) as well as a more specialized form of analysis involving geographic data (in which a circle with a 1-mile radius from the location of the hotel is temporarily created and the names of all restaurants located within this circle are determined).

They enable firms to refine their business analysis. But they also introduce special DBMS needs.

Unfortunately, relational DBMSs weren't originally built to accommodate custom data types and custom forms of analysis. As a result, some firms opted to store specialized data in systems tailored to those needs. Examples include a Geographic Information System (GIS) for managing geo-spatial data or a text retrieval system for managing documents.

Again, early relational DBMSs weren't built with this in mind.

But answering business questions that require access to data managed by multiple such systems often requires an extensive programming effort. Keeping the data in sync is also difficult. And as more and more nontraditional forms of data become critical, the complexity required to make all this work becomes intolerable. Many firms are looking for better options.

But using separate systems for special data can present its own problems.

The World Wide Web

A third factor affecting relational DBMS products is the explosive growth of the World Wide Web. Web browsers have brought a wide range of users online, affording companies a new venue for communicating with their customers, suppliers, business partners, and employees.

The Web is also creating new DBMS pressures.

Web pages contain "unusual" data and Java applets.

This communication is achieved through Web pages constructed using the Hypertext Markup Language (HTML). A single page may contain text, audio, image, animated graphics, and even video data. Typically, pages contain links to other related pages. Some may contain Java applets—software written in the Java programming language that is automatically downloaded from a Web server and run in the user's Web browser to perform a given function. And some pages provide for user interaction, such as filling out a form to search for a specific topic.

The pages themselves also need to be managed effectively.

Again, we see the introduction of "unusual" data types into a business environment. And although Web pages can be easily created and stored as HTML files (with their referenced Java applets, images, audio clips, and other data usually stored separately), doing so can pose challenges as the number of Web pages grows. Recovery, security, and integrity are just a few issues that need to be addressed when managing large numbers of Web pages. Sound familiar? It should. These issues were among those tackled by relational DBMS products, although the focus of such products was on other types of data.

Which Way to Turn?

The recent changes in the IT landscape—including the emergence of object-oriented technology, the need to integrate "specialized" types of data with more traditional business data, and the rapid growth of Web-based computing—create difficulties for users and vendors of relational DBMSs. It seems the industry needs a way to effectively manage *all* types of data and support *all* popular application development platforms—a sort of *universal* database management system.

Can such a system really be built? If so, can relational DBMSs evolve into this role? Or does the industry really need a "new DBMS for new times," as some have argued?

Different approaches have been taken to resolve these problems.

The Revolutionary Approach

The revolutionary approach calls for a new DBMS—perhaps one based on a new data model—to be developed from scratch to address shortcomings associated with traditional relational DBMS products. Proponents of this approach, although not always in agreement with one another, usually express one or more of these views:

- It's too difficult—and too costly—to retrofit the required changes into a relational DBMS.
- The extensive modifications required would take too long. The IT community can't wait.
- Performance is likely to suffer. Relational DBMSs perform well for certain types of applications that work with certain types of data. There's no evidence to show that relational DBMSs can be enhanced to perform well with new forms of data requiring new forms of analysis.

One approach calls for new products built from scratch.

Proponents argue that existing products can't be enhanced without making too many compromises.

- Relational DBMS vendors really don't understand the nature of object-oriented technology. They'll never overcome the mismatch between object-oriented languages and SQL.

- Tables are nice, but they're not enough. It's important to support more complex structures. Relational DBMSs can't do this.

- Relational DBMS vendors are too focused on other problems—like getting their systems to support larger and larger databases as well as more and more users. They don't have the time or interest to take on the broader issues discussed here.

- The only way to ensure things are done *right* is to design a new DBMS with the right requirements in mind.

Revolutionary products haven't broadly succeeded.

These ideas prompted some software professionals to form new companies and develop new DBMS offerings of various sorts. We'll take a look at some of these approaches a bit later. But these approaches have succeeded only within comparatively small market niches, although early commercial implementations appeared as long as a decade ago. Reasons for this vary depending on the product and underlying technology in question. But lack of compatibility with existing systems, lack of complementary tools and applications, the need for extensive user training, poor performance for conventional business applications, limited scalability, and buggy code are shortcomings cited for many revolutionary products in this area.

The Evolutionary Approach

The alternative is to improve what we have.

The evolutionary approach calls for working with—or building upon—existing relational DBMS products in some way. Universal DBMSs generally fall into this category, and we'll talk in detail about them throughout most of this book. Most of the enhancements featured in universal DBMSs aim to make the system more flexible and extensible. Of course, universal DBMSs aren't the only evolutionary approach possible, and toward the end of this book (in Chapter 10) we'll discuss some alternatives.

Arguments in favor of evolving relational DBMSs to fulfill the changing IT requirements described earlier include the following:

- Firms have invested significantly in relational DBMSs. Why not enable them to capitalize on this investment in new ways?

- Relational DBMSs are the result of decades of research and development efforts. They've proven to be reliable, they can handle large amounts of data and large numbers of concurrent users, they run on many platforms, and they meet many critical business requirements. It's unrealistic to expect new products to be able to do the same for years to come.

- Many object-oriented concepts can be applied within a relational environment, without compromising the DBMS. To think otherwise demonstrates a lack of understanding of the relational data model and/or DBMS technology in general.

- By using an evolved version of a familiar system, firms can leverage existing staff skills. They also don't need to worry about having to maintain and integrate yet another system into their IT environment.

- DBMSs alone aren't enough. End user tools, administrative facilities, programming tools, and ready-made applications that work with a DBMS are all necessary. How long will it take for new products to secure a wide range of complementary software from third parties?

- Many relational DBMS vendors have a substantial financial base, ensuring that they can provide their customers with high levels of service and future product enhancements. Unless revolutionary products come from large vendors, the long-term risk is quite high.

Proponents see a means to leverage existing skill and proven technology into new markets.

Not surprisingly, the evolutionary approach is proving more popular than the revolutionary approach.

Universal Database Management Systems Arrive

Universal DBMSs are evolutionary.

To help their customers cope with increasingly complex business needs, many relational DBMS vendors are evolving their products into "universal" DBMSs. Unfortunately, not all products that bear the "universal" name are the same. But fortunately, there is usually some degree of commonality.

They blend object and relational technologies to provide extensible systems.

In general, universal DBMSs seek to support a wider range of data types—the *universe* of data types, if vendor marketing literature is to be believed. And universal DBMSs try to support a broad range of analytic functions for those data types. To do so, many object-oriented concepts are often incorporated, such as enabling users to define their own data types and functions that operate on those types. Thus, in most cases, universal DBMSs are derived from relational DBMSs. They are enhancements to a relational code base that has typically been in use in industry for years.

The enhancements, however, can be quite substantial and affect multiple components of the DBMS. To a large degree, these enhancements represent a blending of relational capabilities with some of the popular concepts associated with object-oriented technology. They're a marriage of sorts, which is why these enhancements are collectively referred to as *object/relational* technology. What this marriage means, in terms of business value and technical features, is the subject of the next chapter.

Summary

An increasingly complex IT environment has prompted many firms to require more from their DBMSs than they were originally designed to support. Greater synergy with object-oriented programming techniques and the ability to effectively manage a variety of "unusual" data types are just two examples of this. DBMS vendors have pursued various approaches to solving these—and other—common business problems.

The majority of this book focuses on an evolutionary approach being adopted by several major vendors and their customers. This approach, based on attempting to "blend" object-oriented and relational technologies, is often marketed as a universal DBMS or an object/relational DBMS. Through Chapter 9, we'll explore what universal DBMS technology is all about and what business value it may bring to the IT community. In Chapter 10, we'll consider alternatives to this approach. And in the final chapters, we'll review ways in which you can determine if the technology is right for you and, if so, how you might begin identifying *your* specific functional requirements and preparing for a successful deployment in your firm.

An increasingly complex IT environment has prompted the advent of 'universal' DBMSs.

We'll explore this DBMS technology in greater detail throughout this book.

We'll also discuss alternate approaches and outline issues that can help you decide if universal DBMSs are right for you.

CHAPTER 2

Merging Object and Relational Technologies

A universal DBMS, as described here, incorporates both object-oriented and relational technologies. The idea is to provide users with a solid database management foundation, yet enable them to customize their environment to suit evolving business needs. This includes supporting new kinds of data, new application development languages, and new ways to analyze the many forms of critical business data that firms possess.

Universal DBMSs can be customized.

For the majority of this book, we'll use "universal DBMS" to refer to systems that are extensible and can treat various forms of data equally. In other words, we'll expect such systems to be "open" enough so that users and third parties can add their own data types and functions. We'll expect these systems not to require separate storage mechanisms, separate server processes, or a separate suite of utilities just to support different types of nontraditional data. We'll expect mechanisms to be provided to ensure reasonable performance. And we'll expect these advanced features to be supported in a manner that is familiar to relational DBMS users—for example, through the use of SQL.

They can store, manage, and integrate many forms of data.

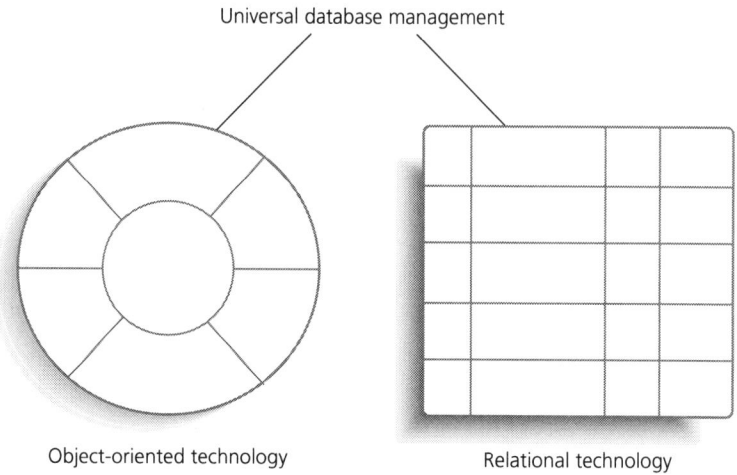

A lot to ask for? Maybe. But some vendors already offer such products, although they're not without limitations.

Moving Beyond Simple Character Strings and Numbers

Relational DBMSs have their own data types.

As we've already discussed, relational DBMS products have their own data type system. This type system supports the forms of data most common to business applications. Integer, decimal, floating-point numbers, date/time, fixed-length character strings, and varying-length character strings are examples of these. But as we've also discussed, business applications increasingly require support for other types of data.

One approach to solving this problem could involve getting the relational DBMS vendors to build support for each new desired type directly into their products. However, this makes IT users dependent on the development priorities, product investment strategy, and general goodwill of their chosen DBMS vendor(s). It also presumes each vendor can accurately anticipate *all* new data type needs for *all* applications developed by its customers and is willing to hire the technical talent necessary to fulfill these needs in a timely manner.

Creating New Data Types

A much more realistic approach to universal database management calls for building a flexible data type system—one that enables users and third-party vendors to add new types as needed. This is the direction universal DBMSs have taken, and commercial offerings are already available that support this function.

Firms must be able to add new types as needed.

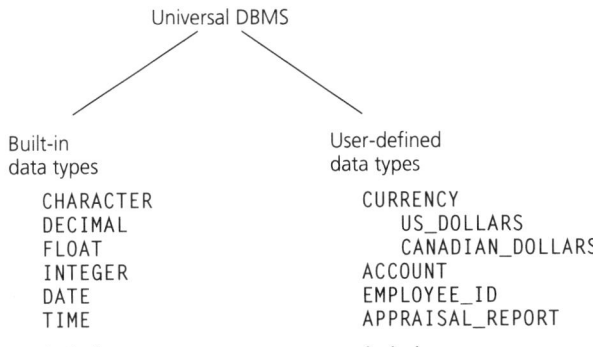

Enabling users to define new types of data is one way in which object and relational technologies are being merged. Object-oriented languages, such as C++, Java, and Smalltalk, enable programmers to define new types or classes of objects by coding statements in that programming language.

Universal DBMSs are borrowing this concept, enabling users to work with new data definition language (DDL) statements in SQL to define new types to the system. If desired, these types can be refinements of existing data types, such as a US_DOLLARS data type based on a built-in numeric data type. Or they can be refinements of other user-defined data types. This draws on the object-oriented concept of inheritance, discussed earlier.

Universal DBMSs support user-defined data types created through SQL.

They borrowed the idea of an extensible type system from object-oriented languages.

Of course, there are differences between the user-defined classes of an object-oriented programming language and a user-defined data type in a universal DBMS. We'll talk about these differences as we delve into user-defined data types in the next two chapters. However, the notion of an extensible type system—common in object-oriented languages—has been adopted by universal DBMS vendors.

Business Value

The ability to extend a DBMS environment to support new types of data brings several business advantages:

Storing new data types in a universal DBMS prevents data from being isolated in many systems.

1. It can minimize the need to store and maintain "unusual" data types in separate file systems or specialized DBMSs. This can simplify systems integration and maintenance issues, as well as ease application development.

2. It enables firms to set their own agendas, building new data types or purchasing ready-made "class libraries" based on their business priorities—not those of their DBMS vendors.

It also helps improve data integrity.

3. It helps firms associate more meaning with their data. In *strongly typed* implementations—something we'll talk about later—firms can ensure that certain nonsensical operations won't be performed, such as directly comparing US dollars with Canadian dollars.

4. It allows firms to leverage their existing investment in relational technology, including existing staff skills.

5. It enables type definitions to be shared by multiple applications, improving overall consistency and eliminating some redundant code.

Recognizing Business Rules

In addition to supporting new types of data, universal DBMSs can be extended to support new kinds of analysis and to automatically enforce site-specific business rules. These capabilities—typically coded as methods in an object-oriented programming language—are implemented through new mechanisms in universal DBMSs. These mechanisms include triggers, stored procedures, and user-defined functions. We'll look at each briefly here, and discuss all in greater detail later.

The DBMS can be instructed to automatically enforce user-defined rules.

Triggers

Triggers are user-written code that "fires" or executes whenever a given database event occurs, such as when a row is changed or deleted. In doing so, the trigger can take appropriate action to ensure that a given business policy isn't violated.

Triggers help ensure local business policies aren't violated.

Examples of business policies include the following:

- Ensure that no managers in the North American sales division receive more than a 7% raise this year.
- For travel expense accounts greater than $5000, record additional information in a special "high expense" tracking table.
- Whenever the inventory for product X falls below 500 units, order an additional 100 units.

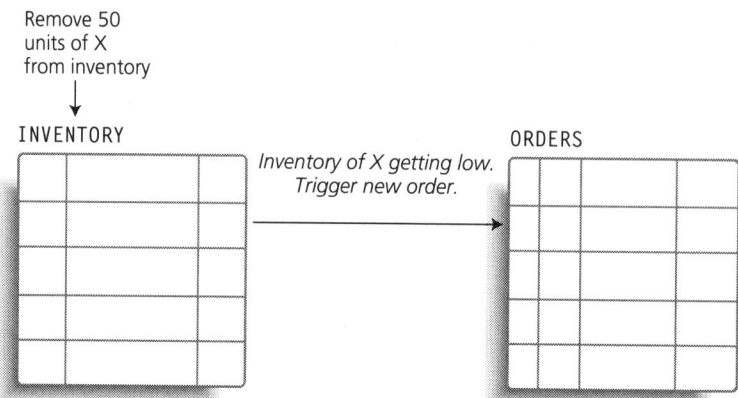

Triggers also minimize redundant application code.

By building intelligence about business policies directly into the DBMS, firms can ensure that uninformed (or malicious) users won't circumvent these rules and possibly compromise important business data. In addition, triggers can prevent the need to code such logic into each of the many applications that might otherwise modify the associated tables in the database. Instead, SQL-based triggers are created once, become part of a user's database, and are automatically executed when appropriate.

In an object environment, trigger services would be written in methods.

Triggers, then, enable universal DBMSs to provide some of the services associated with methods in object-oriented environments. Triggers make the DBMS more "active," capable of automatically taking appropriate action when something happens. And they help firms associate more meaning with their data.

Of course, triggers aren't entirely equivalent to object-oriented methods. But that's something we'll talk about in a subsequent chapter.

Stored Procedures

Like triggers, stored procedures are user-written code that resides on the same system as the DBMS itself. However, stored procedures differ from triggers in several ways. First, they're not automatically executed when something happens to a table. Instead, they're executed when a user or an application specifically invokes them. Second, they're often coded to accept multiple input parameters. And third, they may return results, such as a set of rows, to the calling application or user.

Thus, stored procedures are more like miniature applications or program modules. They often contain multiple SQL queries to read data from or write data to one or more tables. And they usually incorporate conditional logic statements, such as if/then/else statements. In some systems, they can even be written in object-oriented programming languages, such as C++ or Java.

Although application programmers can invoke one or more procedures, they don't need to understand the details of what the stored procedure has been written to do. Instead, they must merely know how to call these procedures (passing in any input parameters needed) and how to process any results returned by these procedures. Because of this, stored procedures help insulate applications from certain database activities and simplify the task of writing portions of the applications.

Stored procedures support code reuse and hide some data access logic.

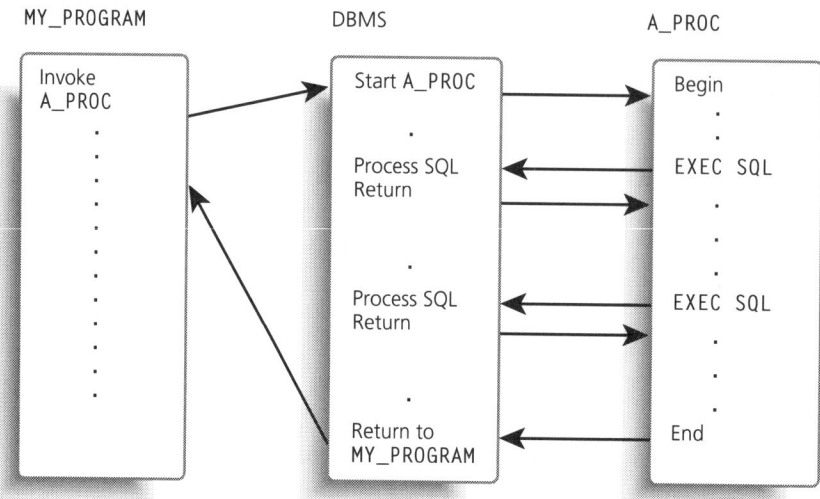

They're also a bit like methods.

In addition, a single stored procedure can be called by many applications. Thus, procedures help promote code reuse. If widely used, they can help define valid operations and services associated with the objects (tables) in a user database. In many respects, then, stored procedures bear some similarity to the methods of an object-oriented environment, much as triggers do.

User-Defined Functions

User-defined functions extend the breadth of SQL.

Just as relational DBMSs originally provided a specific set of data types, they also provided a specific set of built-in functions that can be invoked in SQL queries. Examples of built-in functions include the ability to calculate the sum or average of various numeric data values stored in a table, to extract a subset of data contained in a data value (such as just the "day" portion of a date), and to return the length of a character string.

And just as the predefined set of data types wasn't always enough to satisfy some business needs, the set of predefined functions also wasn't always enough. Universal DBMSs enable firms to create their own functions and incorporate these functions into otherwise standard SQL queries.

The ability to do this is particularly important as new data types are added to the system because new data types often introduce the need for new functions so the data can be analyzed effectively. Recall the geographic analysis discussion from the last chapter. Users might want to query about the distance between two points (perhaps the airport and a hotel) or determine if an object (an Italian restaurant) is within a given area (a 1-mile walking distance of a hotel). To express such queries easily in SQL and enable the DBMS to perform the necessary search operation, new functions need to be introduced—such as "distance" and "within" in these examples.

New functions are often required by new data types.

Object-oriented programmers will recognize that these user-defined functions sound somewhat similar to—but again not entirely the same as—methods. Both facilitate code reuse. Both can be used to help define valid *behaviors* or operations to be performed on specific data. Although differences exist between object-oriented methods and user-defined functions, we again see how universal DBMS products are adapting object-oriented concepts to provide a more flexible overall environment.

These functions support new operations on various types of data.

Business Value

Collectively, the functions we've discussed here offer several business advantages:

- Greater potential for code reuse, eliminating the need to redundantly code certain integrity-checking logic and data access logic into multiple applications. This saves time and reduces both development and maintenance costs.

- Support for new operations (SQL-invoked functions) that work with both traditional and nontraditional data types. These can

Code reuse, support for new forms of business analysis, and greater synergy with object technology are potential benefits.

enable new forms of business analysis, such as geographic analysis, that would otherwise be difficult or impractical to implement.

- Better mechanisms to bridge between an "object" view of the world and a relational view of the world.
- The ability to leverage existing SQL skills.

Supporting Flexible Table Structures

> **Some DBMSs relax typical table structures.**

The ability to create new types and new functions are important ways in which universal DBMSs help integrate object concepts into the relational base on which they're built. However, we've also noted that object-oriented programming languages enable new classes of objects to employ a variety of internal structures—arrays, linked lists, and various sorts of collections (some of which can act as tables). When objects referenced in an application are highly interrelated, it's sometimes more intuitive—and quicker—to use non-tabular structures.

Some DBMS researchers and vendors have experimented with variations on the traditional table structure to address certain performance or data modeling concerns. Often, the underlying focus involves ways to minimize or eliminate the need to *join* data from multiple tables to satisfy a user's request, as joins are an expensive relational operation to execute.

Rows with Multivalue Columns

> **They may store multiple values in one column of a row.**

Among the newer tabular structures sometimes supported by universal DBMSs are those with multivalue columns and complex data types. With multivalue columns, a single column of a row can contain multiple data elements, such as a set of skills for an employee or a set of awards conferred to a student. Thus, the column can contain a *collection* of data elements rather than a single data element. We'll discuss collections in greater detail in Chapter 6.

EMPLOYEE#	NAME	JOB	SKILLS
A10198	P. T. Girle	IT Staff	C UNIX Web
F708651	Hal Yun	DB Admin	RDBMS SQL Win NT
C153290	Herschel Kay	IT Staff	C++ Java

Complex Data Types

Rows with complex data types can have columns that possess an internal structure. Instead of containing just a single, simple data value, these columns may be comprised of data values that have several attributes ("fields"), each of different types.

For example, a PROJECTS table might have several columns, including one for the project owner. OWNER might be defined as a complex data type that contains attributes for the name, job title, and phone number of the responsible party. Systems that support such structures typically provide a means to access and manipulate the embedded attributes, as we'll see later.

Or they may store data that contains its own internal structure.

```
PROJECTS
| ID | DEADLINE | BUDGET | ------ OWNER ------ |
|    |          |        | NAME | TITLE | PHONE |
```

Other forms of "unusual" table structures may also be supported, including nested tables and tables containing rows that possess references—or explicit relationships—to rows of other tables. We'll talk more about some of these unconventional table structures in Chapter 6.

Business Value

Such structures offer greater synergy with object-oriented languages.

The introduction of these—and other—unusual table structures has sparked debate in the DBMS community. Some argue that certain extensions violate key principles of the relational data model and should be avoided. Others claim they can be implemented without any such violations.

Those who favor "relaxed" table structures cite the following advantages:

- Greater flexibility for database design, allowing real-world objects to be represented more readily at the database level

- Greater synergy with object-oriented programming languages, which support various types of objects that employ various forms of underlying data structures

- Potential performance improvements for certain applications

Ensuring High Performance

While a flexible, extensible DBMS might sound good, it's not worth much if performance is poor. To ensure reasonable performance, certain internal components of the DBMS must be changed to become more "open" or customizable.

Sacrificing performance for function won't work.

Indexing one or more columns of a table can speed searches for many queries. Traditionally, relational DBMSs have employed a particular type of index—a B+-tree index or close derivative—that can improve performance for many decision support queries. Such indexes are multilevel, balanced structures that are particularly good at speeding searches involving a range of data values ("Give me the names of all employees who earn between $100,000 and $125,000 per year").

Instead of scanning each page of the table to check for rows that satisfy the search criteria, a relational DBMS might read a small number of index pages to obtain key values of salaries that fall within the range. With each matching value is the corresponding location of the row (in the form of a row identifier, or RID). In this way, the appropriate data rows can be located without reading through the whole table, much as the index of a book can prevent the reader from having to scan the entire text to determine where a given topic is discussed.

Custom Index Structures for New Data Types

New data types often call for new indexing structures.

However, it's well known that B+-tree indexes can't speed performance for all kinds of inquiries involving all forms of data. This is why more specialized systems, such as text retrieval systems and Geographic Information Systems, employ different indexing techniques. A universal DBMS, then, must be prepared to do the same. So in addition to supporting new types of data, new types of functions, and new types of integrity mechanisms, a universal DBMS needs to accommodate new types of index structures.

Realistically, new index structures are most likely to be introduced by third-party vendors who build class libraries for universal DBMSs rather than by IT organizations. The code to implement new index structures can be complicated to write, requiring more of an investment than many IT groups are willing to make.

Enhanced Optimization

Adding new types of indexes impacts the DBMS optimizer.

But regardless of who develops the code, it's important that the DBMS can support it. And supporting it means more than just allowing new types of indexes to be created and stored. It means understanding when they should be used—something that affects the DBMS optimizer.

As you are probably aware, relational DBMSs rely on an internal component—the optimizer—to evaluate access strategies that can be employed to satisfy a user's request. Strategies might involve using one or more indexes defined on a table or avoiding index use altogether in favor of a full scan of the table. By assessing the relative costs of workable alternatives, the optimizer selects an inexpensive one for execution. It's important, then, that parties who develop and integrate new indexing technologies into a universal DBMS environment be able to educate the optimizer about their use.

Indexes for Functions

Finally, we've seen that indexes have been traditionally defined for one or more data columns of a table. This works well when the search criteria reference data in indexed columns. But when the search criteria involve user-defined functions, performance may be improved if indexes can be defined on the output of these functions. For example, a function defined to work with image data may return a value signifying the degree to which a given color or pattern is present in the image. If this function were frequently used as a search criteria, indexing its output could improve performance.

And we probably want to index not just data columns but the output of new functions as well.

In addition, enabling administrators to educate the optimizer about execution costs associated with user-defined functions is also useful. This helps the optimizer make a more accurate cost estimation, which, in turn, can yield a more effective data access strategy.

Business Value

The value of supporting user-defined indexing and optimization extensions include the following:

- Potential for better performance.
- Ability to make better use of DBMS server resources.
- Support for new types of applications and business analysis. Without reasonable performance, certain queries might simply take too long to execute, rendering them impractical and/or unaffordable.

Indexing and optimization enhancements can improve performance and resource usage.

Leveraging Ready-Made Class Libraries

Class libraries provide for code reuse and help cut labor costs.

One particularly appealing aspect of object-oriented programming is the ability to create a number of new classes of objects. These classes can be packaged in libraries that can be readily reused by others. Programmers can create new objects and use associated methods to work with these objects. Java, for example, contains many built-in classes that provide for such useful functions as working with window elements, building applets that can be downloaded for execution into Web browsers, handling exceptions, working with (character) strings, and so on.

Many are already available commercially.

Universal DBMSs support a similar concept, in which user-defined types, user-defined functions, and other facilities can be employed to build database class libraries. A number of third-party software vendors have already built class libraries for particular DBMS products. Like their object-oriented programming language counterparts, these class libraries support generic functions of use to a variety of applications or a specific set of functions useful to particular industry segments. Examples include text and geo-spatial libraries (useful for many industries) and a fingerprint library (useful primarily for law enforcement).

Business Value

These libraries can decrease development and maintenance costs as well as shorten application development time.

Using ready-made class libraries for a universal DBMS offers business advantages that include the following:

■ Reduced in-house development and maintenance costs.

■ Reduced time to implement any applications dependent on new data types and functions included in the library.

■ Ability to leverage skills of specialists outside the company at a reduced cost. Instead of hiring expensive specialists to build a custom library, firms can purchase ready-made libraries at a cost savings.

Summary

Universal DBMSs incorporate many object-oriented concepts within a relational DBMS context. Most implementations build on proven strengths of relational products to offer firms greater flexibility and support new types of business analysis. There's no precise definition of what constitutes a universal DBMS (and, indeed, vendors sometimes use the "universal" moniker to describe products that are far from identical). However, it's common to find that universal DBMS products support several or all of the functions described here: user-defined data types, user-defined functions, triggers, stored procedures, user-defined index structures, and optimization extensions. Collectively, these features provide for a more flexible, active DBMS environment—one that is capable of supporting many forms of critical business data in an integrated and efficient manner.

Universal DBMSs are flexible and provide an integrated way to manage various forms of data.

CHAPTER 3

Managing New, Simple Data Types

As we've mentioned, a key goal of universal DBMSs is to be able to effectively store, search, and manage unusual types of business data. We've already seen examples of why text, image, geographic, and other nontraditional data types represent data that is critical to many businesses. In this chapter and the next, we'll focus on how universal DBMSs offer an *extensible* type system to help firms manage a broader range of business data than more traditional DBMSs do. We'll start our discussion by looking into large objects and simple forms of user-defined data types.

Universal DBMSs provide several ways to manage nontraditional data.

But a few notes are in order before we begin. As much as possible, the universal DBMS approach described in this book is based on the emerging International Organization for Standardization (ISO) "SQL3" specification. If you're not familiar with SQL, don't worry—all examples are explained in plain English. However, in some cases this book discusses specific commercial implementations to illustrate advanced features or fill in for areas where standards activities are still the subject of considerable debate.

Supporting Large Objects

Large objects support unstructured data.

A large object is a data type that allows a single column of a row in a table to contain a large amount of data, typically up to 2 GB. By contrast, relational DBMSs that don't support large objects typically have a limit of 2 KB to 32 KB.

They're suitable for some multimedia types.

By relaxing this size restriction and allowing for data types of much greater length, universal DBMSs can more readily store certain forms of multimedia data, such as documents, image, audio, and compressed video. However, the contents of these large objects are considered to be unstructured by the DBMS. In other words, if someone stored a business report as a large object, the DBMS wouldn't be able to distinguish between the title page, sections within the body of the paper, or the index.

Large objects are usually defined to contain binary data or character data. These two forms of large objects are sometimes referred to as BLOBs and CLOBs, respectively. In most implementations, multiple columns within a single table may contain large objects.

Here's how we can create a table with two different kinds of large objects.

The following example shows how an EMPLOYEE table might be defined to store both traditional and nontraditional forms of business data. The ID column stores employee ID numbers as integers, the NAME column stores employee names as varying-length character strings, the RESUME column stores employee resumes as 1 MB character large objects, and the PHOTO column stores digitized employee photographs as 10 MB binary large objects.

```
CREATE TABLE EMPLOYEE
(ID      INTEGER,
 NAME    VARCHAR(50),
 RESUME  CLOB(1M),
 PHOTO   BLOB(10M))
```

Storing Large Objects

To the user, large objects are stored much as any other type of data. That is, users still write an INSERT statement to add new rows with large objects to a table. Similarly, DELETE and UPDATE statements are still used to remove rows with large objects and to change the contents of rows with large objects.

However, a number of systems can store data in a special manner for performance and administrative purposes. In these systems, large objects are stored on pages separate from the rest of the row containing more conventionally sized data. These pages may be logically grouped in a separate structure and placed on a separate device. This enables administrators to fine-tune the placement of their data, putting critical data on high-speed devices and less critical data on lower-speed devices.

Some DBMSs offer storage options for administrative reasons.

To correlate large objects with other data in the row, such systems usually store a reference or descriptor to the large object within the row itself. For the EMPLOYEE table shown earlier, a number of rows might be stored on the same data page or block. (Physical page size varies depending on the DBMS and operating system in question.) Each EMPLOYEE row on that page would contain the ID and NAME data, as well as pointers to the RESUME and PHOTO data stored separately.

Working with Large Objects

In some respects, DBMS users can treat large objects much as they do other data types supported by the system. That is, they can add large object columns to existing tables, as well as read and write large objects. In some implementations, a number of SQL operations can be performed, such as concatenating two large objects (useful for text data) or determining the length of a large object.

Large objects are manipulated through SQL.

But a number of restrictions apply.

However, the sheer size and nature of large objects has forced vendors to impose certain restrictions that don't apply to other data types. For example, it's common that large objects may not be the subject of "greater than," "less than," or equality comparison operations. Similarly, they may not be used to force query results to be ordered in a certain fashion. They may not be indexed. They may not be defined as *primary* or *foreign* keys.

Primary and foreign keys are associated with the relational data model and are used to enforce *referential integrity*. Briefly, a primary key consists of one or more columns that guarantee the uniqueness of each row in a table. A foreign key consists of one or more columns that reference a previously defined primary key. Values of a foreign key are a subset of the values defined for the corresponding primary key. The combination of primary/foreign keys provides for referential integrity constraints, such as ensuring that insurance claims are opened only for valid policy holders. To do so, a `CLAIMS` table might contain a foreign key column of `POLICY#`, which references the primary key column of `POLICY#` in the `POLICY` table.

If you're getting the impression that large objects require some special treatment, you're right. Indeed, other restrictions on large objects may apply, depending on the DBMS in question. However, large objects *do* enable firms to manage both traditional and nontraditional data types in a single environment. This makes it easier to relate these two forms of data. And when large objects are used as the target of user-defined functions, they can provide greater value. We'll be talking about this when we discuss user-defined functions in a subsequent chapter.

Tuning for Performance

Introducing large objects into a DBMS environment can cause performance concerns. Moving large amounts of data between the DBMS and an application can be very expensive—particularly if the application is running on a separate system than the DBMS, as might be the case in a two- or three-tier environment. In addition, keeping log records for changes to large objects can also introduce substantial overhead.

Since large objects often range up to 2 GB, performance is a big concern.

But without reasonable performance, the value of large objects is questionable. What mechanisms, then, are available to cope with the performance concerns that arise? We'll explore how some universal DBMSs address this issue here. In Chapter 9, we'll also discuss a mechanism called *file links,* which some firms prefer to use instead of large objects partly because of performance issues.

Saving network bandwidth and reducing I/O. Some products support an application programming mechanism (a large object *locator*) that allows large objects to be retrieved in pieces and defers transfer of large objects until absolutely necessary. Doing so minimizes network communications in multitier environments as well as reduces I/O activities on the DBMS. Even in single-machine environments, locators can help minimize unnecessary data movement.

In networked environments, being able to retrieve large objects in pieces can save bandwidth.

Piecewise retrieval can be particularly important when applications wish to operate on only portions of a large object, such as the first 10 KB of a 100 MB document or the first 2 MB of a 300 MB audio clip. Transferring the entire contents of the large object would require unnecessary disk I/O by the DBMS, waste network bandwidth, and consume unnecessary application buffer space.

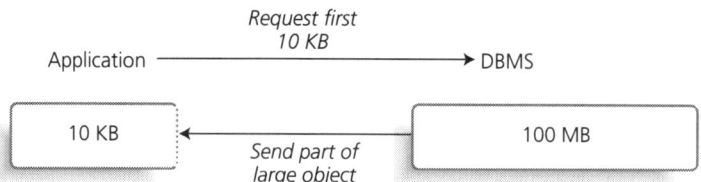

In some cases, deferring data transfer can help as well.

Deferring transfer of large objects can also help conserve network resources and minimize I/O processing. Such deferral calls for programmers to be able to manipulate large objects through SQL expressions without causing the contents of these large objects to be transmitted until the results of the SQL activities are assigned to an application buffer (in a *host variable*) or written to the database. Host variables are used in embedded SQL applications to contain data retrieved from the DBMS or data to be input to the DBMS.

To understand when deferring data transfer might be useful, consider a situation in which one application wanted to select part of one document (stored as a large object), select part of another document (stored as a different large object), concatenate these two document pieces together, append some additional text stored in an application buffer, and finally insert this data as part of a new row into a table based on the results of some test. Using locators prevents any data movement from occurring until the data actually needs to be inserted as a new row in the table. If the test were negative and the insertion didn't need to occur, no data movement at all would be required.

Locators themselves are simply values used in an application to represent large objects. They're not pointers, and they don't actually contain the data within the large object. They're merely a convenient means for programmers to reference individual large objects.

Conserving memory. When working with large objects, memory use is also a consideration. With traditional forms of data (such as numbers and character strings that are typically 4 KB or less), data is passed from an application buffer to a DBMS buffer or vice versa. But handling large objects in the same manner can pose a problem for applications running on machines where memory is constrained.

Some DBMSs provide a way to conserve client memory when large objects are involved.

To avoid the need for applications to allocate large amounts of memory to read large objects from, or write large objects to, the DBMS, some products instead allow data transfers to occur directly between the DBMS and a file. Through the use of a *file reference* or comparable mechanism, programmers can transfer image, audio, or other large object data directly from a file for input into the DBMS. Similarly, they can instruct the DBMS to retrieve large object data and write it directly to a file accessible to the application instead of requiring that it be written to a buffer (memory area) of the application.

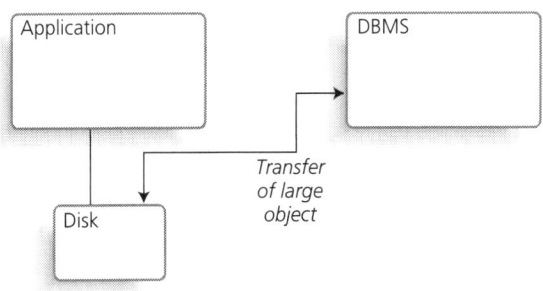

Reducing Log Activities

Finally, the size of large objects introduces logging concerns. As you may be aware, multiuser DBMSs maintain log records to track the write activities of transactions. Both "before image" and "after image" copies of the data are recorded in the log. That is, the log reflects what the data looked like before it was changed as well as after it

Large objects can strain the DBMS log.

was changed. These log records are then used to resolve certain problems that may occur, such as recovering from a media (disk) failure. Thus, a transaction that changes the database in some way—inserts new data, deletes existing data, or modifies existing data—will cause write activities to the log file as well as to the data page(s).

Obviously, adding, deleting, or updating large objects can cause substantial write activity to the log. Moreover, frequent activity of this nature can cause the log to run out of space—an activity that can freeze or hang the entire DBMS until disk space is cleared for logging activity. Given that some DBMSs have a 2 GB file limit for logs, this can render logging of large objects impractical.

Some products make logging optional to reduce I/O activities.

Universal DBMSs often allow administrators to turn off logging of large objects to reduce I/O and thereby improve performance. This option may be specified when the table is created. For example, the EMPLOYEE table could be created to preclude logging of its two large object columns. Here's how we might do so using the syntax supported by IBM's DB2 Universal Database.

```
CREATE TABLE EMPLOYEE
(ID      INTEGER,
 NAME    VARCHAR(50),
 RESUME  CLOB(1M) NOT LOGGED,
 PHOTO   BLOB(10M) NOT LOGGED)
```

Instead, a shadowing technique is used to ensure transaction consistency.

When logging of large objects is turned off, the DBMS must still enforce transaction consistency. That is, while the transaction is in progress, it still must retain the ability to either apply (COMMIT) the data changes or ignore (ROLLBACK) the data changes. To do so, a *shadowing* technique is typically implemented. Shadowing calls for the changed data to be written to new data pages. The original pages—the "shadow"—are retained until the transaction completes. In this way, there's no need to record changed data in the log. If the transaction is committed, the DBMS can discard the shadow and use the new data pages. If the transaction is rolled back, the new pages can be discarded and the shadow used instead.

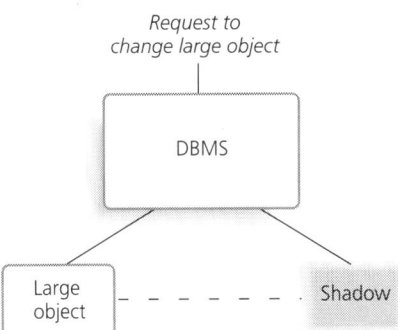

What do you give up by not logging data? It's the ability to recover beyond the time of your last backup in case of a media failure. When a disk crashes, administrators begin the recovery process by restoring data from the most recent backup copy available. Then, the work of committed transactions that occurred after that backup can be reapplied by invoking some DBMS command that initiates *roll forward* or *forward recovery* processing. Such processing relies on log records to determine what data changes need to be reapplied to the database. If these log records don't exist for large objects, their subsequent data changes will be lost. The DBMS may instead set values to these large objects in some arbitrary fashion to reflect this loss (such as setting the values to binary zeros).

However, you do give up something by not logging changes to large objects.

Creating New Types of Simple Data

In addition to large objects, universal DBMSs also support user-defined types. Enabling users to define new data types to the system provides for an extensible environment and helps the DBMS capture more of the meaning that people naturally associate with different forms of data. You'll sometimes see vendor literature refer to this feature as a "UDT," or user-defined data type.

Another way to cope with unusual data is to define your own data types.

Two basic forms of user-defined types are typically supported: simple types, which are derived from a single type already supported by the system (such as integer or character string), and complex types, which contain an internal structure whose attributes consist of multiple data types. We'll focus first on simple forms of user-defined types. In the next chapter, we'll discuss complex types.

New data types are tracked in the DBMS catalog.

However, it's worth mentioning that whenever a new type is created—either a simple or complex type—it immediately becomes available for use. User-defined types are tracked in the DBMS *catalog*, a set of tables containing information about the data that the system is managing. Thus, when someone attempts to reference a user-defined type created previously, the DBMS will check the catalog, find the necessary information, and proceed.

Simple Types

Simple types are based on a single system data type.

Simple data types—sometimes called *distinct* types—are the most basic form of user-defined data types. They enable users to create a new data type based on a single, system-supplied type. While they can be used to merely call a known data type by another name, they're more commonly used to define new types that have a different *behavior*—or different set of valid operations—from the types upon which they were based.

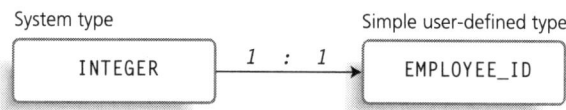

Operational restrictions can vary between the simple type and its base type.

For example, an administrator may want to create an EMPLOYEE_ID data type based on the native integer data type. While both would store numeric data, they would each be treated as different data types by the DBMS. Furthermore, different sets of behaviors can be defined for each. While we might want to allow two integer values to be added together, it doesn't seem to make much sense to allow this operation to be performed on two EMPLOYEE_ID values. Thus, user-defined distinct types help capture more of the semantics people naturally associate with different types of data.

Example. The following statement creates an EMPLOYEE_ID data type based on the system-supplied integer data type. It further specifies that this is the "final" form of this new type. In other words, we can't create subtypes based on EMPLOYEE_ID. We'll talk about subtypes and inheritance in a subsequent chapter.

```
CREATE TYPE EMPLOYEE_ID
AS INTEGER
FINAL
```

Once this type is defined, tables can be created that contain one or more columns of this type. For example, an EMPLOYEE table can be created with columns for ID (an EMPLOYEE_ID), NAME (a varying-length character string), JOBCODE (an integer), and MANAGER_ID (an EMPLOYEE_ID).

```
CREATE TABLE EMPLOYEE
(ID          EMPLOYEE_ID,
 NAME        VARCHAR(50),
 JOBCODE     INTEGER,
 MANAGER_ID  EMPLOYEE_ID)
```

For example, we can create an EMPLOYEE_ID type based on integer data.

And we can create tables that use this type.

ID	NAME	JOBCODE	MANAGER_ID
423	Richard Buck	19	503
987	Bill Virginia	17	123
873	JoAnn Holloway	19	503
503	Hal Yun	18	999
441	Renee E. Ratte	19	123
123	Louise Galdieri	18	999
...	...	...	...

We can specify what users can and can't do with this type.

In addition, we can identify which functions and operators are valid for this data type. For example, we can declare that comparison operations (greater than, less than, equal to) are valid for EMPLOYEE_IDs but that arithmetic operations (addition, subtraction, etc.) are not.

Integrity Implications

The DBMS won't treat our EMPLOYEE_ID type the same as an integer.

Thus, user-defined types carry some important integrity implications. First, even simple user-defined types are treated differently by the DBMS from the built-in types on which they were based. Thus, EMPLOYEE_IDs are considered to be inherently different from integers. This supports the notion of *strong typing* common in certain programming languages.

Strong typing provides for greater levels of data integrity. It enables firms to specify the behavior—or valid operations—for the new types that users create. It also helps ensure that certain nonsensical operations don't occur.

For example, consider the EMPLOYEE table as we previously defined it. Assume that we've instructed the DBMS that comparison operations for EMPLOYEE_IDs are to be allowed, but arithmetic operations are not. (In Chapter 5, we'll see exactly how functions and operators can be defined for new data types. For now, just assume we've done the appropriate work.)

We might say that arithmetic operations don't apply to EMPLOYEE_IDs, but comparisons do.

Because of this, the DBMS will ensure the following:

And the DBMS will automatically enforce these operational restrictions.

- Values of the ID and MANAGER_ID columns cannot be subjected to arithmetic operations, even though their EMPLOYEE_ID type definition was based on an integer data type (for which arithmetic operations are valid). This means that the DBMS will prevent users from adding two ID values together or multiplying a MANAGER_ID value by the constant 2.

- ID and MANAGER_ID values can be directly compared with one another. But neither ID nor MANAGER_ID values can be directly compared with JOBCODE values. Direct comparisons between values of the same type, such as EMPLOYEE_ID, are permitted. Direct comparisons between values of a user-defined distinct data type and any other data type are not. Again, this prevents a nonsensical operation from occurring, as an employee's ID and job classification are inherently different things.

Type Casting

Occasionally, though, a user might want to actually treat one data type as though it were another. This is a well-known concept in programming languages and is called *type casting*. For example, a user might want to compare an EMPLOYEE_ID value to a constant numeric value, perhaps to retrieve the names of all employees who work for the manager whose ID is 123.

Type casting allows us to temporarily treat values of one type as though they were values of another.

```
SELECT NAME FROM EMPLOYEE WHERE MANAGER_ID = 123
```

With a universal DBMS that supports strong typing, such a statement would *not* be valid. That's because the statement involves a direct comparison (a comparison for equality) between an EMPLOYEE_ID value and a constant integer value. But obviously, we need to provide some way to allow users to make this kind of inquiry, as well as others of a similar nature.

This is valuable in certain contexts.

The solution is to allow a user or programmer to temporarily cast a value of one type as that of another type. Often, the DBMS will automatically create casting functions when a new distinct type is created. These functions enable values of the distinct type to be "cast back" into the type from which they were derived, as well as allow values of the native type to be cast as values of the distinct type. So in our EMPLOYEE table, EMPLOYEE_ID values could be cast as integers, and integer values (including constant integers, as shown in the previous query) could be cast as EMPLOYEE_IDs. The resulting query might be written as

For example, we might want to test if an EMPLOYEE_ID value is equal to an integer.

```
SELECT NAME FROM EMPLOYEE
WHERE MANAGER_ID = EMPLOYEE_ID(123)
```

This casts the constant integer value "123" as an EMPLOYEE_ID so that it may be compared with values in the MANAGER_ID column of the table.

If that seems odd to you, think of what would happen if strong typing weren't supported. User-defined distinct types would essentially be treated the same as the system-supplied types from which they were derived. The unique behavior (operational restrictions) and semantics associated with the user-defined type would be lost. So strong typing provides some important integrity features, and to do so means that casting between different data types is necessary.

Summary

We've examined two ways in which universal DBMSs may support unusual forms of data that are simple and unstructured. Large objects are suitable for storing unstructured forms of data that typically range up to 2 GB. Examples include image, audio, and compressed video. And a simple user-defined type is one that's derived from a single, system-supplied type. But the DBMS recognizes it as inherently different and treats it accordingly. These user-defined types can be useful for capturing the real-world semantics of certain business data, such as the fact that employee numbers or product identifiers are inherently different from simple integers.

Large objects and simple user-defined data types are two ways in which universal DBMSs help firms manage unusual data.

Potential advantages of these simple extensions to the DBMS type system include

- a more manageable IT environment, as more forms of critical business data can be handled by a single DBMS
- a means to associate more meaning with data and capitalize on additional mechanisms to promote integrity of data operations
- simplified data access, as a single interface—SQL—becomes the means of working with multiple forms of data
- greater flexibility

But the new data types we've discussed here are only part of the story. In the next chapter, we'll explore how new forms of complex data—data with its own internal structure—can be supported.

We'll discuss more options in the next chapter.

CHAPTER 4

Working with Complex Data

While large objects and simple user-defined types can be useful for certain applications, they don't address the full range of business needs. That's because they work best for managing new forms of unstructured data.

In this chapter, we'll explore more complex forms of user-defined types. Such types can have their own internal structure, consisting of attributes or "fields" based on other data types. In a subsequent chapter, we'll see how to build hierarchies of these types—a mechanism that supports incremental refinement and offers new database design options.

Let's focus on how universal DBMSs enable firms to define more complex forms of data to the system.

What Is "Complex" Data?

While distinct types are useful for capturing the semantics associated with simple data, some situations call for data types with more complex internal structures. Indeed, complex types are more typical of what we find in object-oriented environments. Seldom is a new class of objects defined that contains only one attribute or data member.

Complex user-defined types can have an internal structure with multiple attributes.

Many universal DBMSs enable firms to create user-defined types that are complex in nature. That is, these types contain multiple attributes, each corresponding to a system-supplied type or another user-defined data type. Products may enable these complex types to be used as

They may be used to define a column or a table.

- the type of a column in a table. Complex types used in this way are sometimes called *abstract data types* (ADTs).
- the type of a table—a new concept introduced by universal DBMSs. Complex types used in this way are sometimes called *row types*.

We'll talk about each of these in subsequent sections of this chapter. As it turns out, the way we define each is the same. But how we use each in our database design is rather different.

Using Complex Types for Column Definitions

In the previous chapter, we reviewed how firms can create new data types based on a single, system-supplied type. This new data type—a simple or distinct type—could then be used as the basis for a column definition.

Firms can also create more complex types and use these for column definitions. But unlike distinct types, complex types can consist of multiple attributes. There are other differences between complex and simple types, but we'll cover those later. For now, let's concentrate on the structured aspect. A reasonable question might involve why such types are necessary.

Using Complex Types for Column Definitions

Let's take a somewhat simple example. Consider how an employee's home address might be represented. In a traditional relational environment, an administrator might define one ADDRESS column as a varying-length character string. This column would contain all address information pertinent to US residents—street location, residence qualifier (such as an apartment number), city, state, zip code. Users inserting new rows into the table or updating existing rows might inadvertently leave some information out, which the DBMS couldn't detect. You see, the DBMS wouldn't understand that the address data actually contains a number of separate fields.

Let's consider a complex data type example involving mailing addresses.

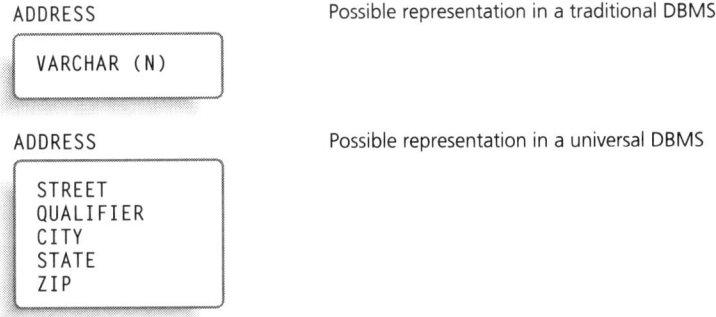

Here are two ways to store mailing address data. The first is as a character string with no structure. The second is as a complex type with specific attributes.

One option, of course, is to break out each address field into a separate column. But this would require everyone who works with employee address data to explicitly include each column in their applications and reports. Doing so is likely to seem counterintuitive to a number of people, who undoubtedly view an "address" as one logical data item and don't want to dwell on its internal structure.

For data types that are more complex than addresses, defining a separate column for each field can be even more confusing. And if a data type actually has attributes based on other complex types, attempts to "flatten" this nested structure can be particularly challenging.

Example

In SQL, here's how we could define a new address data type.

With a universal DBMS, firms may have the option of defining a new ADDRESS data type with multiple attributes. This data type can form the basis for a column in the EMPLOYEE table, as well as columns in other tables.

```
CREATE TYPE ADDRESS AS
(STREET       VARCHAR(30),
 QUALIFIER    VARCHAR(20),
 CITY         VARCHAR(20),
 STATE        CHAR(2),
 ZIP          INTEGER)
INSTANTIABLE
NOT FINAL
```

Let's look at this new type definition more closely. The first line specifies that a new ADDRESS data type is to be created. The subsequent lines within parentheses specify the attributes for this type. In this example, all attributes are based on built-in data types for simplicity; other user-defined data types (either simple or complex) could have been used, if desired. You'll see that the first three attributes are varying-length character strings representing the street location, residence qualifier (possibly an apartment number), and city. Finally, information about the state and zip code are stored as a fixed-length character string and an integer, respectively.

The last two lines of this type definition are optional and will be discussed in Chapter 6. They have to do with type inheritance, an important mechanism employed by universal DBMSs to enable firms to refine and extend their existing data types. But briefly, INSTANTIABLE specifies that instances of this type can be created. In other words, we can store address data in tables that contain a column of type ADDRESS. NOT FINAL specifies that we can create subtypes of this data type if we wish to do so later.

With this new data type created, we can now define tables that contain one or more columns based on the ADDRESS type. The following example creates a new EMPLOYEE table with columns for the employee's ID, NAME, HOME_ADDRESS, and JOBCODE. Note that HOME_ADDRESS is of type ADDRESS, which is the new complex data type we just defined.

```
CREATE TABLE EMPLOYEE
   (ID            EMPLOYEE_ID,
    NAME          VARCHAR(50),
    HOME_ADDRESS  ADDRESS,
    JOBCODE       INTEGER)
```

Now, tables can be created with columns of this new data type.

ID	NAME	HOME_ADDRESS					JOBCODE
		STREET	QUALIFIER	CITY	STATE	ZIP	
. . .	. . .			. . .			. . .
. . .	. . .			. . .			. . .

Of course, since ADDRESS is a user-defined data type with its own internal structure, we need to consider how we'll work with this data. Such capabilities aren't built into traditional relational DBMSs and weren't originally specified as part of SQL. Let's look at how SQL has been extended to support this new concept.

We'd work with this table using SQL.

Working with Columns That Contain Structured Data

If you're familiar with SQL, you know that it includes statements for manipulating data in tables. These data manipulation statements provide for inserting new rows in a table, deleting rows from a table, selecting rows from a table, and updating rows in a table.

These same statements are supported for rows that contain columns based on complex data. But because these complex data types have an *encapsulated* internal structure, universal DBMSs introduce new functions that must be incorporated into SQL data manipulation statements. Doing so means that the internal structure of the data type is not directly exposed to users and programmers. Instead, individuals invoke these functions, which in turn understand the type's internal structure and can perform the necessary work on the user's behalf.

> **But to guarantee encapsulation, the DBMS provides special functions or interfaces to our complex data.**

Three types of functions are typically associated with complex data types when they are used to define columns of tables: constructors, observers, and mutators. Default functions of each type may be created automatically by the universal DBMS. Here's a brief explanation of each of these functions:

- **Constructor functions.** A constructor enables you to create a new instance of the data type. Typically used when inserting a new row into a table, a constructor accepts data values as input. It then populates each attribute of your data type with the appropriate data value so the information can be stored in a table. Constructors in universal DBMSs are much like constructors in object-oriented programming languages, which are used to create object instances of a given class.

Using Complex Types for Column Definitions

- **Observer functions.** An observer function is used for retrieving or reading data contained within the data type.
- **Mutator functions.** A mutator function is used for changing data within the data type.

While we won't delve into every aspect of how to use these functions, it's worthwhile to review a few examples.

Inserting rows. As we just mentioned, a *constructor* creates a new instance of a complex data type. Doing so enables the instance to be inserted as part of a new row in a table. Consider the EMPLOYEE table we just created, with its columns for the employee ID, NAME, HOME_ADDRESS, and JOBCODE. You'll recall that the HOME_ADDRESS was based on our ADDRESS complex data type.

> One function enables us to create new "instances" of our data type.

To insert a row into this table, we'll write a standard SQL INSERT statement. But part of this INSERT statement will include a call to the "address" constructor function. In object-oriented programming languages, new types or classes of objects have constructor functions that share the same class name. Universal DBMSs adopted the same notion.

> We create instances so we can insert them into rows.

The following example inserts a new row into the EMPLOYEE table with information about John Blake. The ADDRESS constructor takes the input values for John's address, constructs an ADDRESS instance, and enables this to be inserted into the table along with the rest of John's employee information. Note that since John doesn't have an apartment number or other residence qualifier, we've specified a null value for that attribute here. Nulls are used in relational DBMSs to represent missing, unknown, or inapplicable data.

> Here's an example of how to construct a new instance when inserting a new row.

```
INSERT INTO EMPLOYEE
VALUES
(14807,
'JOHN BLAKE',
ADDRESS('1501 MAIN ST.', NULL, 'SAN JOSE', 'CA',
        95125),
12)
```

ID	NAME	HOME_ADDRESS					JOBCODE
		STREET	QUALIFIER	CITY	STATE	ZIP	
14807	John Blake	1501 Main St.	null	San Jose	CA	95125	12
...	...	...	...	...	...	...	...

Likewise, we use a function to retrieve elements within a complex type.

Retrieving data. As you may be aware, data retrieval is accomplished in SQL through the SELECT statement. The SELECT statement is still used to retrieve data from tables in universal DBMSs, even if those tables contain one or more columns based on complex data types. However, SQL3 calls for observer functions to be used to access attributes within a complex data type. This preserves the notion of encapsulation.

Let's consider a query in which we want to retrieve the names of employees who live in the state of New York or whose zip code is 95125 (a particular area of San Jose, California). To do so, we need to invoke the observer functions supplied by the DBMS to work with the various attributes of the ADDRESS data type.

For each attribute, an observer function reads in the value based on the type on which it was defined. Thus, the STATE observer function will return a CHAR(2) string. If this string is "NY" (for New York), the employee name will be included in the result set given to the user. Similarly, the ZIP function will read integer values representing zip codes. If the zip code is "95125", the employee name will also be included in the result set.

Here's an example of how we'd query a table based on the values of two particular attributes of our type.

```
SELECT NAME
FROM EMPLOYEE
WHERE STATE(HOME_ADDRESS) = 'NY'
OR ZIP(HOME_ADDRESS) = 95125
```

A shortcut sometimes supported by universal DBMS vendors involves the use of *dot notation*. This notation is merely shorthand for invoking the observer functions. For those familiar with navigating through a data structure, this notation may be more intuitive.

Some DBMSs support an alternate syntax that uses a dot notation. It accomplishes the same thing.

Dot notation involves the use of the column name and attribute name of the complex type. Thus, HOME_ADDRESS..STATE refers to the STATE attribute of the HOME_ADDRESS column. Here's the way we could write the same query using dot notation.

```
SELECT NAME
FROM EMPLOYEE
WHERE HOME_ADDRESS..STATE = 'NY'
OR HOME_ADDRESS..ZIP = 95125
```

Some products use a single dot notation (HOME_ADDRESS.STATE) rather than the double dot notation shown here. As of this writing, the SQL3 standards work in this area has not been finalized.

Finally, we also use a function to change elements within a complex type.	**Changing data.** Just as observer functions enable users to retrieve attribute values of complex data types, mutator functions enable users to modify attribute values of complex data types. Again, doing so preserves the notion of encapsulation.

Mutator functions may be provided by the system for each attribute of a complex data type. As input parameters, each expects a column name and a value for the attribute. |
| **Here's an example of how we might do that.** | Let's imagine that John Blake's zip code was changed by post office representatives to 95111. To update the EMPLOYEE table, we could issue the following SQL statement:

```
UPDATE EMPLOYEE
SET HOME_ADDRESS = ZIP(HOME_ADDRESS, 95111)
WHERE ID = 14807
```

It may be easier to read this query from the bottom up. The WHERE clause specifies the employee number for John Blake. The SET clause invokes the ZIP mutator function. Since HOME_ADDRESS was defined as a column of type ADDRESS, it contains a ZIP attribute and a corresponding ZIP mutator function. Here, we're replacing the current value of the ZIP attribute in John Blake's address with a new integer value of 95111. The first statement, of course, specifies that we want to update something in the EMPLOYEE table. |
| **Again, some DBMSs enable us to achieve the same result using a dot notation.** | As you may have guessed, we can also use dot notation for mutator functions. Here's another way we could have changed John Blake's zip code data.

```
UPDATE EMPLOYEE
SET HOME_ADDRESS..ZIP = 95111
WHERE ID = 14807
``` |

Again, in some products a single dot notation is used rather than the double dot notation shown here.

Advanced Issues

We've discussed the basics of how complex data types can be used to define columns of a table. But as you may have guessed, there's more. A complex data type can contain attributes based on other complex data types, supporting embedded data structures. Complex types can also be extended and refined over time by building type hierarchies and making use of inheritance. We'll address both of these issues in Chapter 6, which focuses more on database design issues.

There's more to complex data types than we've covered here.

But now's a good time to explore another way in which administrators of universal DBMSs may be able to employ complex data types. This involves using complex types as the basis of table definitions.

But let's turn now to their use in table definitions.

Using Complex Types to Define Table Structures

Complex data types can also be used to define the structure of the rows to be included in a table. In relational DBMSs, a table definition always involves specifying a number of columns and their associated data types. In a universal DBMS environment, administrators may create tables in the same way, but they have a broader range of data types to choose from when defining the columns of their tables.

However, an administrator of a universal DBMS may also be able to create a table consisting of complex types. When used in this manner, each attribute of the complex type becomes a column of the table. Rows of the table become instances of this complex type.

Each attribute of the data type becomes a separate column in the table.

This provides new modeling options and synergy with object-oriented languages.

Why would anyone want to do this? Using complex types in this manner provides an administrative convenience: they enable multiple tables to be created that share common characteristics. But they do more than just that. They also offer a new means for modeling data relationships that's perhaps more intuitive to object-oriented programmers. And they can be used to construct table hierarchies, extending users' ability to manipulate data in new ways.

Example

Consider our EMPLOYEE table, and let's assume we need to track projects each employee is working on.

Let's consider an example of when we might want to define a table based on a complex data type. Perhaps our database needs to keep track of projects that employees are working on. In a relational environment, we'd probably store the project data in a separate table from the employee data and join these tables when we wanted to find out specific data about various projects that employees are working on. Of course, we could store project data along with employee data in a single table, but doing so compromises certain database design principles and is best considered on an exception basis.

In a universal DBMS environment, we have the same options just described. We can also define a complex data type for PROJECT and use this as the data type of a new column in the EMPLOYEE table. But this still compromises certain relational database design principles. And it also means we may have lots of duplicate PROJECT data stored in our EMPLOYEE table, as many employees typically work on a single project.

Another option available to some universal DBMS administrators is to define a table based on a complex data type and reference rows that are instances of this type. Let's see how this works.

Using Complex Types to Define Table Structures

The following example defines a new complex data type for projects. We've named this type PROJECT_TYPE and defined attributes for the project ID, code name, description, and budget.

```
CREATE TYPE PROJECT_TYPE AS
(ID            INTEGER,
 NAME          VARCHAR(20),
 DESCRIPTION   VARCHAR(50),
 BUDGET        INTEGER)
 INSTANTIABLE
 NOT FINAL
```

Here's how we can create a complex data type for projects.

However, how we're about to use this type in our database design is very different. We're going to create a table to contain instances of this type. In other words, we'll define a PROJECT table containing rows that have columns that match the attribute names and data types specified for our new data type. The following example does so.

```
CREATE TABLE PROJECT OF PROJECT_TYPE
```

This type will be used in a different way in our database design.

PROJECT

ID	NAME	DESCRIPTION	BUDGET
480	Starburst	Extensible DBMS prototype	10,000,000
...	...	...	...

Instead of using it to define a column, we'll use it to create a table that will contain instances of this type.

Once we've done this, we can query the table using standard SQL (without any SQL3 extensions). For example, the following query will return data about all projects whose budget exceeds $1 million. Note that we're not invoking any special functions to access the data (as we have to do when working with complex data types that form the basis for columns). That's because there's no notion of

And we'll query this PROJECT table using standard SQL.

encapsulation for complex types when they're used to define the structure of rows in a table. Instead, attributes are exposed as columns in tables. Encapsulation only applies when a complex type is used as the definition of a column.

```
SELECT *
FROM PROJECT
WHERE BUDGET > 1,000,000
```

Creating References to Complex Types

But being able to define a complex type, create a table of this type, and query the table in a traditional way isn't really all that interesting. What is interesting about complex types used as table definitions is that administrators can define a new column to serve as a reference to instances of these types. Doing so assigns a value to each row that is unique within the database. This value never changes as long as the row exists. If you're familiar with the concept of an object identifier (OID), these references are a bit like that, except in some implementations, firms have the option of generating their own unique reference values or allowing the DBMS to do so automatically.

But we can also define references to rows in the PROJECT table.

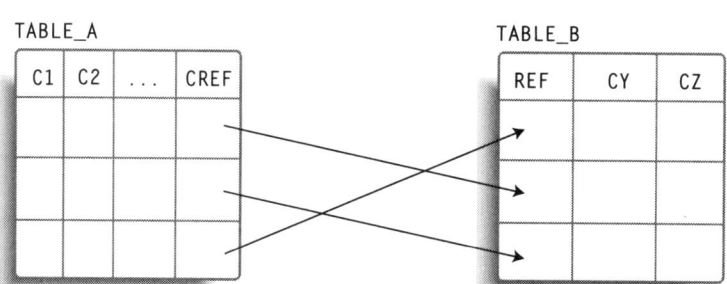

Each row in one table can explicitly reference a row in another table.

What's so good about references? Well, they provide a new way of modeling relationships among data in multiple tables. And they provide for greater synergy with object-oriented programming languages (such as C++ and Java), at least at a conceptual level. You see, object-oriented programmers often define classes that contain pointers or references to other objects. Here, we see a universal DBMS mechanism that enables one row in a table to reference another row in the same or a different table.

C++, Java, and other programmers are familiar with the concept of a reference.

This may all be a bit clearer if we consider an example. Let's reconsider our PROJECT table and define it in a slightly different way. Specifically, we'll add a new PROJ_REF column. This column will contain a reference—a unique identifier—for each row in the table. The value of each reference will be generated automatically by the DBMS. The scope of this reference is the PROJECT table and any subtables defined upon it. We'll discuss the issue of subtables a bit later.

Here's how we can modify our PROJECT table definition to support references.

```
CREATE TABLE PROJECT OF PROJECT_TYPE
(PROJ_REF    REF(PROJECT_TYPE)
     VALUES ARE SYSTEM GENERATED
     SCOPE OF PROJECT_REF IS PROJECT)
```

PROJECT

PROJ_REF	ID	NAME	DESCRIPTION	BUDGET
xxxxxx	433	DB2	Universal DBMS	20,000,000
...	...	...	...	...

Now, related tables can contain references to specific PROJECT rows.

Now we can create an EMPLOYEE table that contains a reference to a specific row in the PROJECT table. This will help us represent a relationship between a specific employee and a specific project. We'll go back to our earlier definition of the EMPLOYEE table and modify it slightly to add the ASSIGNMENT column that will contain the reference to the employee's current work project.

```
CREATE TABLE EMPLOYEE
    (ID             EMPLOYEE_ID,
     NAME           VARCHAR(50),
     HOME_ADDRESS   ADDRESS,
     JOBCODE        INTEGER,
     ASSIGNMENT     REF(PROJECT_TYPE) SCOPE PROJECT)
```

This helps capture data relationships.

The design we've just showed here supports *m:1* relationships. That is, many employees can be associated with (or reference) the same project. In a later chapter, we'll see how row types and references can be combined with *collection types* to help model *1:m* and *m:n* relationships.

Note that this example also illustrates how multiple forms of user-defined types may be associated with a single table. Here, we've used a complex type (ADDRESS) as the basis for a column that will contain information about the employee's home address. Earlier in this chapter we created this data type. This table also contains a column based on a REF (or reference) data type. This particular reference is to instances of rows in the PROJECT table, which was created based on the PROJECT_TYPE that we defined earlier. And, of course, our ID column is based on the simple user-defined EMPLOYEE_ID data type we created in Chapter 3.

Using References to Access Data

Let's consider how queries are written when we have a database design that uses references and tables based on complex types. Suppose we want to determine the names of all employees who work on the project named "Stargazer." The following example shows how this query could be written.

```
SELECT E.NAME
FROM EMPLOYEE E
WHERE E.PROJ_REF -> NAME = 'STARGAZER'
```

> **It also allows for path expressions, which let users "navigate" through our interrelated tables using SQL.**

The first two lines specify that values for the NAME column in the EMPLOYEE table (abbreviated by the variable E) are to be returned. The final line specifies the search condition using a *path expression*. It tells the DBMS that we're only interested in employees who work on projects of a specific name. The DBMS will follow the references in the EMPLOYEE table to specific rows in the PROJECT table. If the project's name is "Stargazer," it will include the employee's name in the result set.

Changes to referenced rows can also be made using path expressions. You may be wondering what happens if a row referenced by another table is deleted. When the DBMS attempts to resolve the reference, it will determine that the target row no longer exists and return a null value instead. To avoid dangling references—or references that "point" to nonexistent rows—administrators can define appropriate referential integrity constraints that will cause the DBMS to set the reference values to null when rows in the target table are deleted.

Some people have a tendency to equate references with pointers or row identifiers (RIDs) that the DBMS can directly use to determine the physical location of the target row. The assumption here is that the use of pointers or RIDs can speed the process of resolving a

> **But don't confuse references with pointers.**

reference, eliminating the need to perform costly join operations for certain queries.

But there are trade-offs with storing RIDs in columns that contain references. Certain operations that require physical movement of data, such as reorganizations or some updates of rows, can create a ripple effect in the database, potentially generating considerable I/O. For example, an operation that required the DBMS to move row X from address A to address B would affect not only the pages containing these addresses but all the pages containing references to row X. The process of determining which pages reference row X, as well as changing all necessary references, could easily become costly.

SQL3 does not take a position on how references are implemented internally by DBMS vendors. At least one major vendor does not store RIDs in columns that contain references.

Referential Integrity vs. References

If you're used to working in a relational DBMS environment, you may be wondering about how references differ from primary/foreign key relationships defined as part of a referential integrity constraint. Although they may seem similar, they're really not the same thing.

References shouldn't be used as a replacement for referential integrity constraints.

According to the SQL standard, a referential integrity constraint can specify inclusion dependencies between foreign key values in one table and primary key values in one or more tables. In other words, an administrator could define column X of table T1 to be a foreign key referencing the primary keys of *both* tables T2 and T3. Thus, foreign keys don't necessarily have a relationship with one row in one table (although many administrators choose to implement their referential integrity constraints as such). By contrast, a reference value always refers to one particular row in the database.

Using Complex Types to Define Table Structures

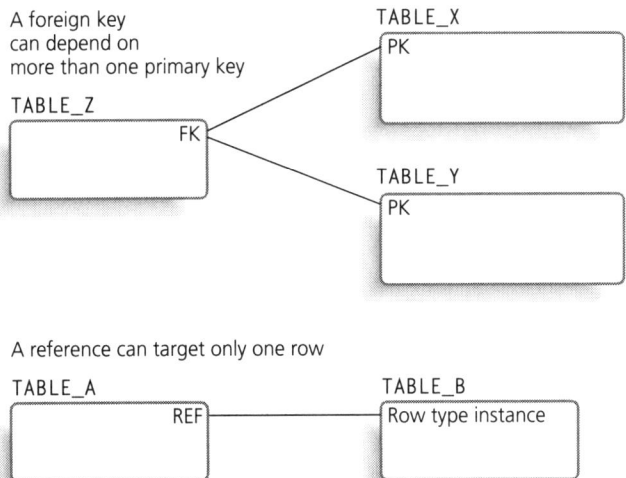

In addition, strong typing isn't automatically enforced with primary and foreign key relationships in commercial products. Thus, a primary key could be defined on one data type, and a dependent foreign key could be defined on another (compatible) data type. References automatically enforce the notion of strong typing. Furthermore, navigational-style SQL access (or the use of path expressions) is supported with references but not with primary/foreign keys. The reason for this is that references uniquely target a specific row. As we see in the previous figure, foreign keys may have dependencies on multiple rows.

On the other hand, references are only applicable to tables defined on complex types. Referential integrity constraints can be defined for *any* data types. They're also an integral part of the relational data model, and their usefulness has been well established for many years. Therefore, references shouldn't be thought of as a replacement for referential integrity constraints but rather as an additional database design mechanism.

Summary

Universal DBMSs provide lots of choices on how to manage unusual data.

In the previous chapter, we saw how universal DBMSs enable firms to create new, simple forms of data—that is, data types that contain no internal structure. In this chapter, we focused on how universal DBMSs may enable firms to create new, complex forms of data—that is, data types that do contain an internal structure.

We've seen two ways in which complex, structured data can be used.

These complex types can be used when defining a column in a table or when defining the table itself. Complex types that form the basis of column definitions are sometimes called *abstract data types*. Complex types that form the basis of table definitions are sometimes called *row types*. When used as the basis of a table definition, complex types enable administrators to create explicit relationships between tables through the use of *references*, a new data type supported by some universal DBMSs. We briefly covered some database design issues in this chapter, and we'll explore that topic later in this book. We also noted that complex data types can be extended and refined over time, using type hierarchies and inheritance. We'll be talking more about that topic in Chapter 6.

Potential benefits of complex type support include the following:

- Greater affinity with object-oriented programming techniques, which enable programmers to create new types or classes of objects that have their own internal structure. This helps bridge the gap between an "object" point of view and a "DBMS" point of view.
- Ability to manage new forms of data and capture real-world semantics.
- Greater flexibility.
- New mechanisms for modeling data relationships.

But data types aren't the whole story. A flexible, extensible DBMS environment calls for firms to be able to build greater knowledge of their business rules and processes directly into the DBMS. Universal products support various mechanisms to do so. We'll look at these in the next chapter.

But there's more to universal DBMSs than new data types . . .

CHAPTER 5

Building Business Knowledge into the DBMS

In the last two chapters, we discussed how an extensible type system allows new forms of data to be stored in a universal DBMS. By enabling users to define their own data types, universal DBMSs can capture more of the meaning—or semantics—people associate with their business data.

In this chapter, we'll explore how firms can build additional knowledge of business policies and processes into a universal DBMS. Doing so makes for a more "active" overall environment, in which the DBMS can automatically take appropriate action when certain events occur. In addition, we'll discuss how firms can create their own functions and operators to further extend the DBMS environment to meet their needs. Often, new functions are introduced to facilitate new forms of business analysis, such as geographic analysis and temporal analysis. Finally, we'll talk about ways to improve performance and facilitate code reuse. Stored procedures are often used to help achieve these goals.

Users of universal DBMSs can build knowledge of business rules and processes into the system.

Enforcing Business Rules Automatically

Various mechanisms are available to support user-defined integrity constraints.

Corporate environments quite commonly have a variety of business rules that affect operations on their data. Some of these rules are simple requirements involving the valid range of values for certain data. For example, employee ID numbers might need to range from 1 to 100000; the sex of an employee might need to be recorded as either "M" or "F"; the corporate divisions in which an employee might work could be "Sales," "Manufacturing," or "Administration"; and so on.

Other rules may be more complex, such as preventing any employee from getting more than a 10% raise or automatically ordering new parts when inventory falls below a certain threshold.

Once defined, these rules are automatically enforced. This reduces application complexity and simplifies maintenance.

In either case, it's important for firms to be able to instruct the DBMS regarding such rules so that critical data integrity constraints can be enforced automatically. Without a sufficiently robust means for doing so, firms would be forced to hard-code enforcement of these business rules into each application that might modify the database. Not only would this decrease programmer productivity, but it would introduce maintenance headaches. A new or modified business policy would require changes to many applications. Failure to make the appropriate changes to a single application could cause the rule to be violated, compromising the quality of the stored data.

To avoid such problems, universal DBMSs typically support *CHECK constraints* and *triggers*. Indeed, these mechanisms were first implemented in traditional relational DBMSs and are examples of early attempts to make such systems more active. Universal DBMSs are building upon these facilities, as well as providing new functions, to further enable firms to push business knowledge into their DBMS products.

Constraints

CHECK constraints provide a simple means to perform data range checking on values input to the DBMS. Such constraints are commonly specified when a table is created to ensure that new rows won't be outside the range of valid data values. Subsequent attempts to change data in the row will also cause the DBMS to ensure the data range constraint won't be violated.

Table-based CHECK **constraints enforce simple data range validation.**

The following example creates an EMPLOYEE table with a SEX column. Associated with this column is a constraint that values must be either "M" or "F."

```
CREATE TABLE EMPLOYEE
(ID      EMPLOYEE_ID,
 NAME    VARCHAR(50),
 SEX     CHAR(1)
         CHECK (SEX IN ('M', 'F'))
)
```

EMPLOYEE

ID	NAME	SEX
...	...	...

Values must be "M" or "F."

More complex CHECK constraints are also supported, such as those that involve Boolean comparisons as well as AND/OR logic. The following example ensures that commissions are given only to employees who work in the Sales division.

These constraints can involve one column or multiple columns of a single table.

```
CREATE TABLE EMPLOYEE
(ID          EMPLOYEE_ID,
NAME         VARCHAR(50),
DIVISION     VARCHAR(20),
COMMISSION   INTEGER
             CHECK (( COMMISSION > 0 AND DIVISION
             = 'SALES') OR
             COMMISSION = 0)
)
```

EMPLOYEE

ID	NAME	DIVISION	COMMISSION
...	...	...	...

Nonzero values permitted only for Sales staff.

Triggers

Triggers enforce complex rules and often involve multiple tables.

Triggers provide a means to enforce more complex business policies, including those that affect multiple tables. Triggers consist of SQL code associated with a given table. When a change to the table occurs, the body of the trigger is executed, potentially causing changes to other tables. In this way, important business rules can be identified to the DBMS once (through the creation of a trigger) and enforced automatically. This reduces application development time and improves code maintenance.

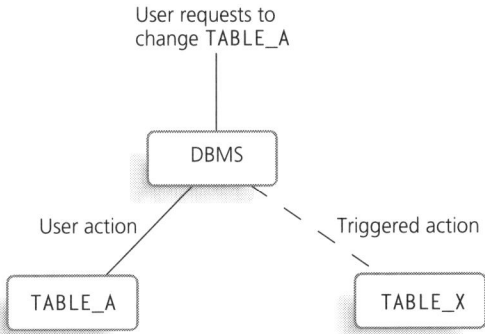

Because triggers first emerged in commercial offerings in the late 1980s and the SQL standard for triggers wasn't created until some time later, different implementations still exist in different products. However, several common characteristics are associated with triggers:

- **The activity or event that causes the trigger to fire.** This can be an attempt to delete a row of a table, insert a new row into a table, or update the values in one or more columns of a row in a table. In any case, it is typically some *write* activity that causes a trigger to fire. (However, at least one vendor also enables triggers to be fired when a read activity occurs.)

- **The time at which the trigger will fire.** Triggers can be written to fire before or after the activity occurs.

- **The granularity of the trigger,** which controls the number of times the trigger will fire per SQL operation. Triggers can be defined to execute once for each SQL operation or once for each row affected by the operation. Thus, if an UPDATE statement affects 10 rows of a table, a row-based trigger will execute 10 times, while a statement-based trigger will execute once.

- **The use of *transition tables* and associated variables,** which provide a way for programmers to reference both the old and new

Firms can control when triggers execute, what they do, and if nested execution is supported.

values of the rows affected by the SQL operation that caused the trigger to execute.

- **The level of nesting or recursion** that's allowed to occur. Because triggers can be written to automatically change other data, they may set off a chain reaction. The work of one trigger could cause another trigger to fire, which in turn could generate work that caused another trigger to fire, and so on. In some circumstances, this could lead to an infinite loop. Therefore, most vendors that support nested trigger execution impose an arbitrary limit on the number of "cascade" actions that can occur. Programmers may also be able to specify that a single trigger should cause no cascading activities.

- **The order of trigger execution.** Most DBMSs allow multiple triggers of the same type to be defined on the same table. This helps keep the trigger bodies relatively small (for easy maintenance). However, having multiple triggers of the same type defined on the same table can lead to logical problems if an administrator or user can't control the order in which these various triggers are executed. Unfortunately, some commercial offerings lack such a control mechanism and warn their users that the execution order is "undefined." If using such a product, the implications of an unpredictable execution order must be carefully considered before defining multiple triggers. In other offerings, execution order can be determined through some simple means, such as the first trigger created of that type will be the first to execute.

> Triggers are best understood by considering a few examples.

Trigger examples. Let's take a look at some examples of triggers to better understand what they can do and how they can be written. In the first example, we'll consider how to enforce a business rule that requires all new requests for reimbursement of travel expenses to contain valid accounting codes, so these expenses can be charged to the appropriate department and project. Unfortunately, few employees remember account codes. They frequently try to file expense reports without them, resulting in reimbursement delays and extra labor. A trigger can avoid this situation without forcing employees to memorize the various account codes.

Assume the DBMS has an EXPENSE table with columns for the employee's serial number, name, department number, project number, travel start date, travel end date, expense total, and account code. Assume the DBMS also has an ACCOUNTING table with the appropriate account code for each project within each department.

We can create a trigger to ensure expense accounts have proper accounting information.

```
EXPENSE TABLE:
    EMPNO, DEPTNO, PROJECT_ID, BEGIN_TRAVEL,
    END_TRAVEL, TOTAL, ACCOUNT

ACCOUNTING TABLE:
    ACCOUNT, DEPT, PROJECT
```

With such a database, a trigger can be created that will fire before a new row is inserted into the EXPENSE table. The body of the trigger can check information in the ACCOUNTING table to determine the appropriate charge code for this expense. This information will then be reflected in the new travel expense record to be inserted into the EXPENSE table.

We might specify that this trigger will execute before any new rows are inserted into an EXPENSE table.

```
CREATE TRIGGER ACCTG_TRIGGER
BEFORE INSERT ON EXPENSE
REFERENCING NEW AS N
FOR EACH ROW
WHEN (N.ACCOUNT IS NULL)
    SET N.ACCOUNT =
        (SELECT ACCOUNT
         FROM ACCOUNTING
         WHERE DEPT = N.DEPTNO
         AND PROJECT = N.PROJECT_ID)
```

We'll read accounting data from another table and be sure this is included in the new row.

Since this syntax may be new to you, let's take a minute to step through the example. The first line creates a trigger called ACCTG_TRIGGER. The second line indicates the trigger will execute before an INSERT operation is performed on the EXPENSE table. New values—contained in the row about to be inserted into the table—will be referenced later in the trigger by N, a transition variable. The trigger will fire once for each row inserted into the table that contains a null ACCOUNT value. Finally, the last several lines set the value of the ACCOUNT column in the new row. This is accomplished by looking up the appropriate information in the ACCOUNTING table, based on the department number and project ID associated with the new row.

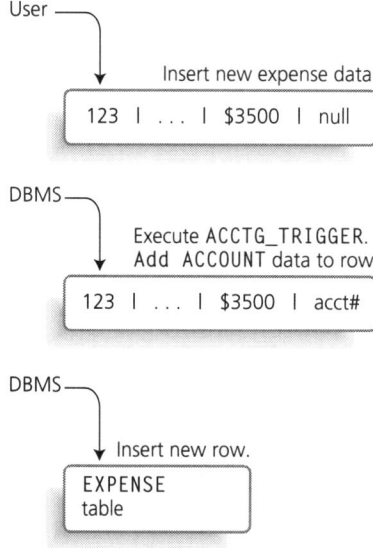

Just as triggers can cause data to be read from other tables, they can also cause changes to be made to other tables. Consider a business rule in which all travel expenses over $5000 must be recorded in a separate table for audit purposes. Again, we have an EXPENSE table in our database, as previously described. In addition, we have a TRAVEL_AUDIT table that tracks the serial number and department number of the employee who filed the expense account, the total of the expense, and the end date of the trip.

Triggers can also write data to other tables automatically.

```
EXPENSE TABLE:
    EMPNO, DEPTNO, PROJECT_ID, BEGIN_TRAVEL,
    END_TRAVEL, TOTAL, ACCOUNT

TRAVEL_AUDIT TABLE:
    EMPNO, DEPTNO, SUM, END_TRIP
```

To ensure that new travel expenses that exceed $5000 are recorded in the audit table, we can create a trigger that executes after a row is inserted into the EXPENSE table. This trigger will read the values of appropriate columns in the new row and cause another row with this data to be inserted into the TRAVEL_AUDIT table.

Perhaps we want to keep track of expensive travel in a special table.

```
CREATE TRIGGER BIG_SPENDERS
AFTER INSERT ON EXPENSE
REFERENCING NEW AS N
FOR EACH ROW
WHEN (N.TOTAL >= 5000)
    INSERT INTO TRAVEL_AUDIT VALUES (N.EMPNO,
        N.DEPTNO, N.TOTAL, N.END_TRAVEL)
```

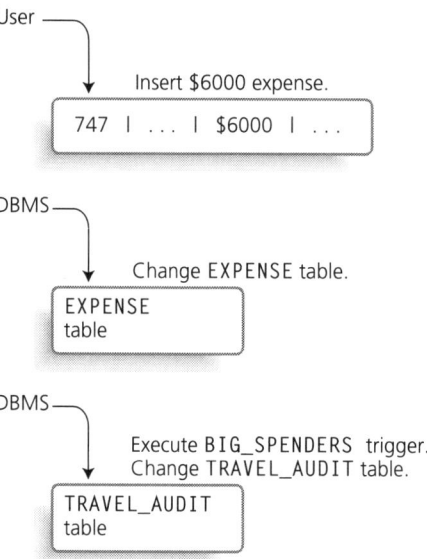

Whenever someone adds a new EXPENSE **row for travel over $5000, we can have appropriate data noted in a** TRAVEL_AUDIT **table.**

Triggers can execute for write operations other than row insertions.

Finally, we'll consider an example of a trigger designed to execute only when someone attempts to update the value of a specific column. In this case, we'll assume a company wants to allow employees to receive an annual bonus of up to 10% of their base salary. Our database contains an EMPLOYEE table with columns for the employee's number, name, salary, and bonus.

```
EMPLOYEE TABLE:
    EMPNO, NAME, SALARY, BONUS
```

We might want to make sure no employee gets a bonus exceeding 10% of the employee's salary.

To enforce the business rule, we could write a trigger that executes before anyone updates values in the BONUS column of the table. (For purposes of this example, we'll ignore the work that would need to be done if someone decreased an employee's salary.) The following trigger checks to see that changes to the bonus amount won't exceed 10% of the employee's salary. If the bonus is within these limits, the update can proceed as usual. If it's not, the trigger will instead set the bonus to the maximum permissible value of 10%.

```
CREATE TRIGGER BONUS_CHECK
BEFORE UPDATE OF BONUS ON EMPLOYEE
REFERENCING NEW AS N
FOR EACH ROW
WHEN (N.BONUS > .1 * N.SALARY)
   SET N.BONUS = .1 * N.SALARY
```

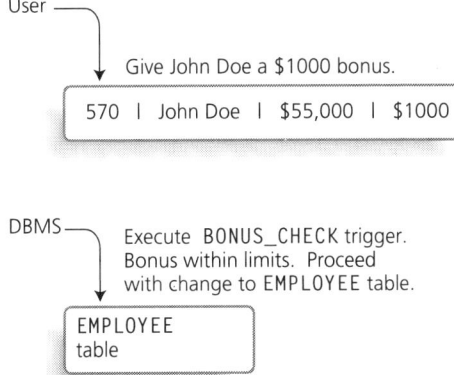

Again, we can write a trigger to check when BONUS values are changed. If the change would exceed 10%, we can take appropriate action.

Trigger considerations. Although triggers are a very popular mechanism for capturing business rules in a DBMS environment, they're not without their downside. In many DBMS implementations, heavy use of triggers can slow performance of certain activities. Any activity that matches the conditions specified in one or more triggers will cause those triggers to execute. This creates additional work for the DBMS, as trigger bodies invariably call for additional read or write activities to be performed.

Triggers are both popular and powerful. But they must be used with care.

They can slow performance and increase system overhead, particularly if they're poorly written.

Careful coding of triggers is essential for minimizing system overhead. Triggers should be defined to fire only when absolutely necessary, and the work they perform should be as restrictive as possible. In some cases, such as during a data import or load phase, it may even be desirable to temporarily disable trigger execution for performance reasons.

There's more to triggers than what we've covered here. But some of the issues are quite specific to given business requirements and DBMS implementations. The main points to remember are these: triggers enable users to build greater business knowledge into their DBMS, triggers facilitate code reuse, and triggers make for a more active and extensible DBMS environment.

Linking DBMS Events to External Events

Firms may also want database events to trigger activities outside the DBMS, such as generating an email message.

Until now, we've concentrated on how knowledge of business rules can be built into a universal DBMS so that new forms of data integrity can be automatically enforced. But sometimes, firms may want a database activity to trigger actions outside the DBMS itself. For example, if someone updates an `EXPENSE_ACCOUNT` table to seek reimbursement for travel expenses exceeding $10,000, a firm might want electronic mail to automatically be sent to the employee's manager and a member of the finance department. Similarly, if the value of a particular stock rises above a certain threshold, a firm might want the system to beep and open a message window on an analyst's workstation.

Event alerters do this.

Event alerters provide a means to achieve such goals. Like triggers, event alerters are associated with a table and automatically execute when a given SQL operation occurs. Unlike triggers, event alerters are designed to generate activities external to the DBMS, such as sending email messages.

Event alerter mechanisms are found in a number of commercial offerings, but their implementation is even less standardized than trigger implementations. One approach, taken by IBM, builds on the trigger mechanism discussed earlier. That is, a programmer creates a trigger that fires based on some database event. After checking certain conditions (that relate to the business rule in question), the trigger may invoke a user-defined function or stored procedure to take external action.

Sometimes they're implemented in nearly the same way as a trigger.

We'll talk in greater detail about user-defined functions and stored procedures later in this chapter. But briefly, they are user-written code stored on the same system as the DBMS server. User-defined functions are invoked within an SQL data manipulation statement. Stored procedures are invoked by an SQL CALL statement (or equivalent). In some implementations, functions and procedures can be written in standard programming languages (such as C) and perform any function valid within that language. Examples include issuing system calls, writing data to a file, generating a beep, and so on. Used in this way, the function becomes a means for the DBMS to automatically force external actions to occur when needed.

Imagine we want to automate reordering of parts when current inventory levels fall below 25% of maximum. And let's assume that automating this process requires taking some action outside the DBMS, such as sending a message to the purchasing organization with information about the current inventory level of the part in question. So our DBMS contains a PARTS table, with columns for part numbers, part descriptions, quantity in stock, and maximum stock level. Someone has also written a NEW_ORDER procedure and defined this to the DBMS. We'll talk about stored procedures and user-defined functions shortly. For now, just assume this procedure contains code that can take input values and do whatever is necessary to get a new order generated.

```
PARTS TABLE:
  PARTNO, DESCRIPTION, IN_STOCK, MAXIMUM

STORED PROCEDURE:
  NEW_ORDER(INTEGER, INTEGER)
```

Here's one example of how we might write an event alerter to automatically cause new parts to be ordered when inventory falls below a certain threshold.

With the `PARTS` table and `NEW_ORDER` function defined, we can create an event alerter on the `PARTS` table that will automatically execute after someone updates the `IN_STOCK` or `MAXIMUM` values associated with a given part. If the change would cause the inventory levels of the part to fall below the maximum threshold, this event alerter will take appropriate action, automatically invoking the `NEW_ORDER` function.

```
CREATE TRIGGER REORDER
AFTER UPDATE OF IN_STOCK, MAXIMUM
ON PARTS
REFERENCING NEW AS N
FOR EACH ROW
WHEN (N.IN_STOCK < .25 * N.MAXIMUM)
   CALL NEW_ORDER(N.MAXIMUM - N.IN_STOCK, N.PARTNO)
```

Customizing SQL to Meet Your Needs

Universal DBMSs also enable firms to customize SQL.

We've already discussed ways in which universal DBMSs enable firms to customize the data types and data integrity constraints supported by their system. In addition to providing considerable flexibility in these areas, universal DBMSs also enable firms to extend the functions supported by SQL.

Relational DBMSs have traditionally supported a limited number of built-in functions to perform operations such as computing an average, calculating a sum, returning minimum or maximum data values, and extracting a portion of data from a character string. But new data types often call for new functions. Recall previous chapters in which we introduced geographic data and wanted to determine the distance between two points or all the objects of one type that are located within a given region.

Indeed, firms may even want to extend the range of functions that can be performed with system-supplied data types. For example, functions for computing the square root, sine, cosine, and standard deviation of a number aren't built into all commercial products. Similarly, functions specific to certain regional areas or industries, such as computing a payroll withholding tax or a hotel room tax, surely aren't built into commercial offerings.

Users can write their own functions and use these in subsequent queries.

Universal DBMSs cope with these situations by enabling firms to define their own functions and operators that can be incorporated into SQL statements. Once defined, these functions and operators can be used in queries just as though they were native functions and operators.

Example

Unfortunately, implementations for user-defined functions vary considerably in commercial offerings. In some cases, user-defined functions are written in procedural or object-oriented programming languages. In others, functions may be written in some form of extended SQL. When programming languages are supported, C is most common, although some products also enable user-defined functions to be coded in C++, Java, and other languages.

Usually, these functions are written in extended SQL or programming languages like C, C++, or Java.

Once coded, these functions are identified to the DBMS through some SQL data definition statement. Again, implementations vary. But the following example shows one way in which a user-defined function can be created to calculate the square root on an integer column. (Some additional specifications are omitted here for brevity.)

Here's how we can define a new function to the DBMS.

```
CREATE FUNCTION SQUARE_ROOT(INTEGER)
RETURNS FLOAT
LANGUAGE C
EXTERNAL NAME '/U/CINDY/BIN/DBMSLIB!SQRT'
. . .
```

The first line identifies the function name (SQUARE_ROOT) and specifies that it expects one integer value as input. Next, we see that a floating-point value will be returned. The code for this function is written in C. And the external name identifies where the code can be found to execute the square root function. In this case, it's part of a library found at "/U/CINDY/BIN/DBMSLIB"; "SQRT" is the entry point in the library for this particular function.

Later, we can invoke this function just as we would any other system-supplied function. The following query will return the square root of values in COL1 for all rows contained in TABLEX.

```
SELECT SQUARE_ROOT(COL1) FROM TABLEX
```

Simple vs. Complex Functions

Simple functions return a single (scalar) value.

Functions themselves may be thought of as simple or complex. Perhaps the simplest type of a user-defined function was illustrated in the previous example: it accepted a single value as input, performed some function, and returned a single value as output. Functions that return a single data value are sometimes called *scalar* functions.

More complex functions return multiple values.

A more complex function might return multiple data values. These can be multiple rows within a table or multiple values related to items outside the DBMS itself. An example of the latter might be a function that accepts an employee name as input (stored in the NAME column of an EMPLOYEE table) and searches an electronic forum or bulletin board for items posted by this employee, returning the record ID and posting date for each item.

Functions that return multiple data values are sometimes called *table* functions because results are returned as though they were rows in a temporary table. However, the process of creating a function is generally the same regardless of whether the function is scalar or table-based.

But the basic process of creating each type is the same.

Performance, Security, and Administrative Issues

Any discussion of introducing user-defined functions into a DBMS would be incomplete without some mention of performance and security issues. A fundamental consideration is where the code for these functions will execute. Execution can occur either in the same address space (or process) as the DBMS or in a separate address space (or process) from the DBMS.

It's reasonable to wonder where these functions will run.

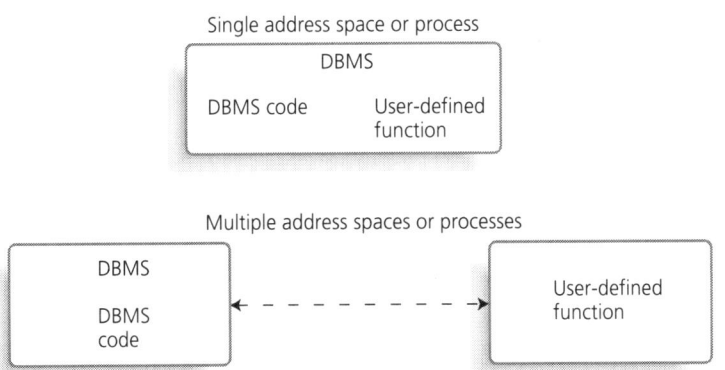

The choices are simple: run them in the same address space or in an address space separate from the DBMS.

Executing a user-defined function in the same address space as the DBMS minimizes system overhead and improves performance. However, it also means that the function could potentially modify or damage internal DBMS memory structures and compromise the system. Some universal DBMSs offer programmers a choice for specifying how their functions are to be run, while others don't. In

The trade-off is performance vs. system security.

general, it's best to run user-defined functions in a separate address space, unless you're absolutely sure the code is bug-free and you need to achieve the highest performance levels possible.

Backup procedures are another issue.

In addition, products that support user-defined functions written in C or some other programming language typically do not store the source code for these functions in the database. They reside in external files. Administrators need to take this into consideration when planning their backup and recovery strategies, as DBMS utilities may not encompass the source files for these functions.

Synergy with User-Defined Types and Large Objects

User-defined functions can complement user-defined types and large objects.

User-defined functions can complement other features of a universal DBMS, such as user-defined types and large objects. They can help define the valid set of operations—or behaviors—associated with new types. In this respect, they're a bit like the methods of an object-oriented environment.

In Chapter 3, we discussed how simple user-defined types (also called *distinct* types) are based on a single, system-supplied data type. For example, an EMPLOYEE_ID data type might be based on integer data, and a US_DOLLAR data type might be based on decimal data. However, strong typing causes the DBMS to treat distinct types differently from the system types upon which they were based.

They define valid "behaviors" or operations.

So, system-supplied operators and functions won't automatically apply to distinct types. In some cases, this makes sense and no further action needs to be taken. For example, adding two EMPLOYEE_IDs together and computing the average EMPLOYEE_ID aren't sensible operations to perform. However, these same operations would make sense—and should be supported—for US_DOLLAR values.

One option is to cast US_DOLLAR values back to their base type before adding them together, computing the average, or performing other operations. But this can be tedious. What we really want to do is declare that various system-supplied functions are acceptable for this particular distinct type. One way to achieve this is to create user-defined functions for these types. But rather than reimplementing these functions in C or some other programming language, we'd like to say that the source code for these functions should be derived from native DBMS functions. Some universal DBMSs offer this ability.

The following example presumes an administrator has created a user-defined distinct type for US_DOLLARs based on a system-supplied decimal data type. Here, the "+" or addition operator is defined to enable two US_DOLLAR values to be added together. Note that the source code for this operator is the "+" operator supported by the DBMS for decimal data types.

Sometimes it's useful to base user-defined functions on system-supplied functions. Here are some examples.

```
CREATE FUNCTION "+"(US_DOLLAR, US_DOLLAR)
RETURNS US_DOLLAR
SOURCE "+"(DECIMAL(), DECIMAL())
```

Similarly, the AVG (average) function commonly supported by relational DBMSs can be defined to apply to US_DOLLAR values. Here, a user-defined AVG function is created for US_DOLLARs based on the system-supplied SQL AVG function.

```
CREATE FUNCTION AVG(US_DOLLAR)
RETURNS US_DOLLAR
SOURCE AVG(DECIMAL())
```

Of course, user-defined functions can add richness to complex data, enabling new forms of analysis and new operations to be performed on that data. Consider a simple geographic analysis problem where a user wants to determine the distance between two points. Assume

Functions can also complement complex types.

a complex data type for points has been defined to the system to record *x, y* coordinates. A function can be created to operate on point data, calibrating the distance between these two points. Here's a simple example.

```
CREATE FUNCTION DISTANCE(POINT, POINT)
RETURNS INTEGER
LANGUAGE C
EXTERNAL NAME '/U/CINDY/BIN/GISLIB!DIST'
. . .
```

Similarly, more complex functions can be defined to perform more sophisticated work with user-defined types, such as determining if one region in space (perhaps a new housing complex) overlaps with or is wholly contained within another (perhaps the projected tolerable driving distance to a shopping mall).

Finally, they can also work with large objects.

In addition, user-defined functions can provide a means to simulate complex data support in systems that otherwise lack this ability. Doing so calls for large objects—unstructured data types that often range up to 2 GB—to be used as "containers" for the complex data. User-defined functions are then created that understand the internal structure of the data within the large object and perform appropriate operations.

A simple example might involve using a large object data type to store information about lines. Each large object of this type might contain four integers—two for the *x,y* coordinates representing the starting point of the line, and two for the *x,y* coordinates representing the end point of the line. The DBMS wouldn't understand the internal structure described here, since large objects are perceived as a series of bits. But functions could be written that interpret the contents of the large object, perhaps computing its length or its midpoint.

However, it's best to use native support for complex data types if at all possible. Doing so can simplify coding requirements, as well as offer improved performance, because knowledge of the data's structure is built into the DBMS itself.

Function Overloading

Allowing firms to create their own SQL functions and operators leads to the issue of *overloading,* a concept introduced by object-oriented programming languages. Overloading means that multiple functions (or operators) can be defined with the same name. The system determines which function is executed by examining the *signature* of the function. In other words, it looks at the arguments passed as input, determines their data types, and executes the function that has a matching signature or set of arguments.

Different functions can share the same name as long as each has different input parameters.

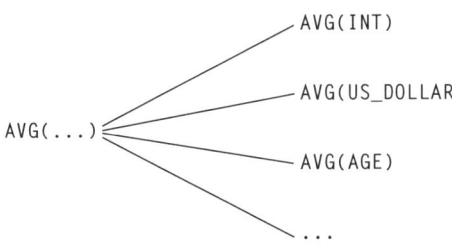

Many universal DBMSs support this capability. Indeed, we've already seen examples of function (and operator) overloading in the previous section of this chapter. The addition operator ("+") and the AVG function were overloaded to work with US_DOLLARs.

We've already seen examples of this.

Perhaps you've already guessed why overloading is a desirable feature. It helps simplify the system for users and programmers. If we didn't have overloading, new function names would have to be created for operations that did basically the same thing, only with different data types. So if we wanted to compute the applicable tax for hotel rooms, clothing, liquor, and cigarettes, we might have

Overloading functions and operators helps simplify the environment for users and programmers.

to learn four different names for each of these four different functions.

It's far easier for users if we create each of these functions with the same name ("TAX") but different input parameters (for hotel room, clothing, liquor, and cigarettes). Then users would only have to learn one function name, and the system would determine the appropriate code to execute by examining the parameters passed to the function as input.

Encouraging Code Reuse

All the mechanisms we've discussed in this chapter—constraints, triggers, event alerters, and user-defined functions—help make for a more active DBMS environment and promote code reuse. Each serves some of the same purpose as the methods of an object-oriented programming language. But there's one more mechanism, introduced by relational DBMSs a number of years ago, that also promotes code reuse, provides some equivalency to methods, and helps improve performance in networked environments. It's a stored procedure, which we'll turn to next.

Stored procedures are similar to miniature applications. They typically contain multiple SQL statements and conditional logic statements. Because they reside on the same system as the DBMS and can be invoked from a remote system with a single network call, they minimize communications overhead and reduce the time for which the DBMS may hold locks on behalf of the transaction. In this way, performance is improved, system resources are used more efficiently, and a greater degree of concurrent access to data can be achieved.

A stored procedure is another useful mechanism supported by universal DBMSs.

Benefits of Stored Procedures

In a traditional DBMS environment, a client application (running on a different system than the DBMS server) would issue a single SQL statement for each request for database services. This resulted in a network call. The DBMS would then return results to the application, making another network call. And the process would be repeated for each SQL statement issued.

Without procedures, clients must make one network call for each SQL statement.

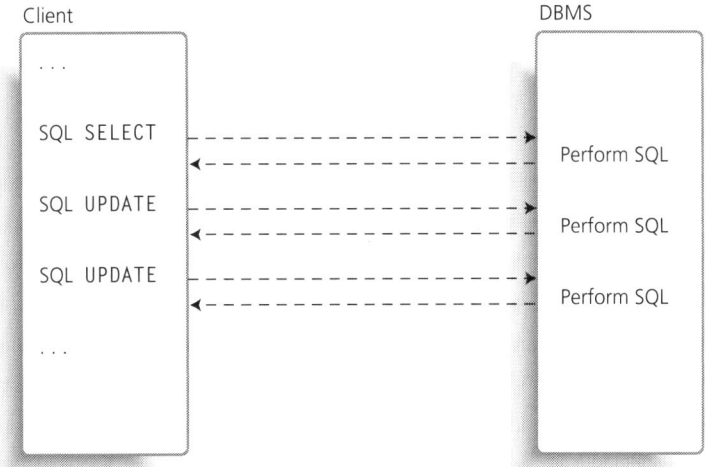

If the statements were all part of a single database transaction (or logical unit of work), the DBMS might need to hold a lock on the affected data until it received an instruction from the client to commit the transaction or roll back its work. If much network I/O were occurring, these locks could be held for a relatively long period of time. And some (or all) of these locks might block the work of other concurrently executing transactions, forcing them to wait.

With procedures, network traffic can be reduced substantially.

Furthermore, contention over resources may be reduced at the DBMS server.

Stored procedures enable programmers to get around this problem by grouping SQL statements into a single module stored on the server. The client application can invoke a procedure with a single network call. Results can also be returned with a single network call. Obviously, this reduces network traffic considerably. It also enables transactions to be processed more quickly (because the DBMS isn't waiting on as many network I/O operations to continue), thereby reducing the duration of time for which locks may be held.

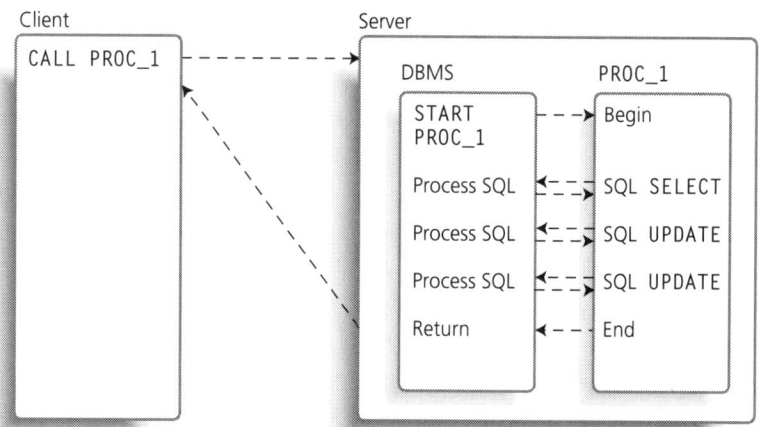

Many SQL statements can be contained in a single server procedure.

Beyond offering performance gains, procedures can encourage code reuse.

But performance isn't the only issue here. Code reuse is another key consideration. Frequently executed database operations can be grouped together in a single procedure, which may be invoked by a variety of applications. This eliminates the need for that code to be written into each application, reducing development time and improving application maintenance. In a sense, procedures provide a means of off-loading some application work from the client platform onto the server.

Writing Stored Procedures

Again, stored procedure implementations vary from product to product. Most vendors enable users to write procedures in one of two ways:

- Through some extended form of SQL
- In a procedural or object-oriented programming language, such as C, COBOL, Java, C++, and so on

As you might imagine, each has its advantages and disadvantages.

Implementations that support purely SQL-based stored procedures are generally easiest to use, since SQL is an easier language to learn than COBOL, C, or the like. However, SQL is also more limited than a programming language. For example, file I/O isn't part of SQL but is built into most programming languages.

To compensate for this, DBMS vendors that support SQL-based stored procedures have extended SQL in certain ways. Common extensions include support for loops, conditional logic statements, and error handling. Some of these extensions are vendor-specific, but a number have recently been standardized. However, these SQL extensions still don't offer the full breadth of function available through a programming language. But they're relatively easy to learn and use. Many individuals without professional programming experience can write their own simple procedures.

Stored procedures written in a programming language are more flexible but require more skill to write. They more closely resemble an application program than an SQL-based procedure. And, as such, professional programming experience is usually required to write and debug such procedures.

Procedures are written in extended SQL or in programming languages.

Extended SQL procedures are generally easier to write.

But procedures written in a programming language can be more powerful.

However, the advantage of such an approach is that these procedures can perform any function that can be coded within the programming language itself, including writing to files, calling operating system functions, or (in some cases) even invoking work involving a second DBMS.

Summary

> We've seen a number of ways in which universal DBMSs can bring rich query capabilities and advanced integrity enforcement to their users.

Universal DBMSs provide a number of ways for firms to build additional business knowledge into the database environment itself. We've covered several common mechanisms here—constraints, triggers, event alerters, user-defined functions, and stored procedures. Collectively, these mechanisms approximate the methods of object-oriented environments, although they're not identical. The chief benefits of using these mechanisms to build greater business knowledge into the DBMS include

- a means to associate more meaning with data, avoiding nonsensical operations or "behaviors"
- automatic enforcement of business rules
- potential for greater code reuse
- potential for improved performance

CHAPTER 6

Modeling Data in New Ways

All our discussions of how universal DBMSs can capture new forms of data and greater levels of knowledge about business rules may have left you wondering about how this will impact database design. Indeed, these new capabilities open up new options for designers and administrators. But there's really more to the story than we've covered so far.

Universal DBMSs introduce new database design options.

Complex data types can be incrementally refined and extended over time. This is accomplished by employing *type hierarchies* and *inheritance,* two mechanisms commonly found in object-oriented programming languages. We'll talk about them in this chapter. Moreover, some universal DBMSs may also support the notion of *table hierarchies,* which we'll also discuss. And finally, some products provide built-in support for *type collections,* such as sets of data or arrays of data. Such collections enable administrators to create tables with multivalue columns or to model nested table structures. We'll explore collections as well.

We can build data type and table hierarchies, as well as use built-in support for collections of data.

Hierarchies and inheritance support incremental refinement.

Refining and Extending Data Types

Inheritance is a highly useful concept integrated into object-oriented programming languages. Programmers working in languages such as C++, Java, and Smalltalk can create new classes of objects based on other classes of objects that have been previously defined. Subclasses inherit the characteristics and behaviors—the attributes and functions—associated with their parent class(es). In this way, inheritance supports incremental refinement, enabling programmers to leverage existing work while accommodating changing business needs. Doing so promotes code reuse. It also helps reduce application development and maintenance efforts.

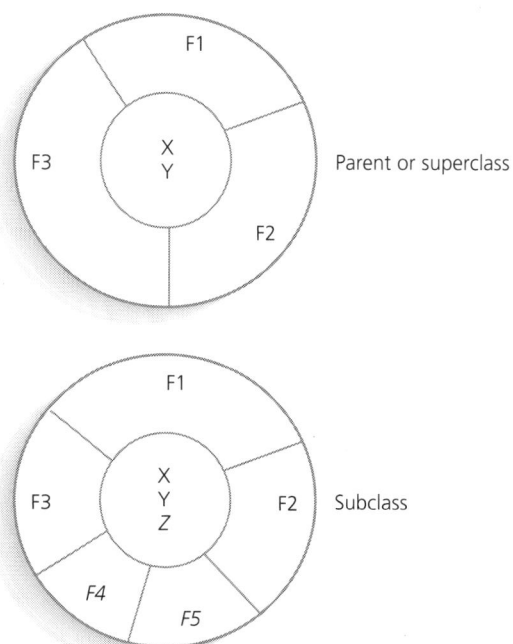

Like object-oriented programming languages, universal DBMSs also support the concepts of inheritance and subtyping of complex data types. Let's revisit some of the complex data types we created in Chapter 4 and consider how we might want to refine them.

Subtyping a Complex Type

A good place to start might be the data type we created earlier for address data. As you may remember, our main objective when defining the ADDRESS type was to capture the basic attributes associated with simple US addresses: street location, qualifier (perhaps for an apartment number), city, state, and zip code. Here's how we had originally defined that data type:

Complex data types can be refined and extended through subtyping.

```
CREATE TYPE ADDRESS AS
(STREET       VARCHAR(30),
 QUALIFIER    VARCHAR(20),
 CITY         VARCHAR(20),
 STATE        CHAR(2),
 ZIP          INTEGER)
INSTANTIABLE
NOT FINAL
```

This structure is quite suitable for storing employees' home addresses, which was our original design objective. However, business addresses can be a bit more complex. In addition to the attributes just described, many firms have an internal routing code that enables their mail room to deliver letters and packages more quickly to their destination. This routing code may be the office number, a department number, or something else.

For example, we can create a new BUSINESS_ADDRESS type based on our previous ADDRESS type.

At first glance, we may want to use the QUALIFIER attribute of ADDRESS for this data. But that's probably not ideal. Many firms have suite numbers or building numbers as part of their addresses, as well as internal routing codes. We might prefer to reserve the QUALIFIER attribute for the former and create a separate INTERNAL_MAIL attribute to accommodate the latter.

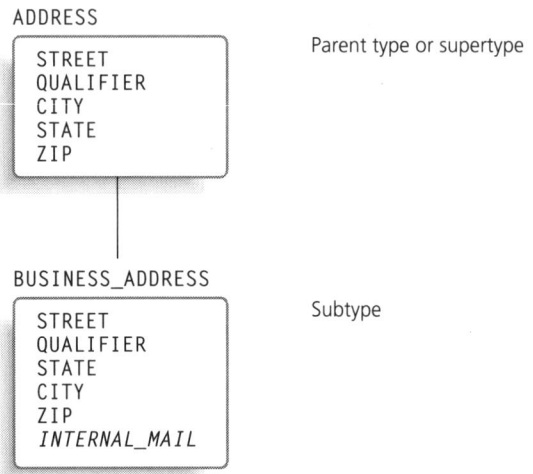

In this example, we've added one new attribute to capture our notion of a business address.

Fortunately, we can do so because the ADDRESS type definition specified that it was NOT FINAL. This permits us to make subtypes of this data type. If we had specified FINAL as part of the ADDRESS definition, no subtyping would have been permitted.

Here's how we can create that new subtype.

Here's how we might define a new BUSINESS_ADDRESS data type that's derived from our ADDRESS data type.

```
CREATE TYPE BUSINESS_ADDRESS
UNDER ADDRESS AS
(INTERNAL_MAIL    VARCHAR(20))
INSTANTIABLE
FINAL
```

The first line specifies that we're creating the BUSINESS_ADDRESS type. The second declares this type to be "under" the ADDRESS type in the type hierarchy. In other words, BUSINESS_ADDRESS is a subtype of ADDRESS. Next, we specify the new attribute associated with business addresses: an internal mail routing code represented by a varying-length character string. The fourth line specifies that this type can be instantiated, or that we can create instances of BUSINESS_ADDRESSes and store these instances in a column of a table. We'll discuss instantiation in greater detail later in this chapter. Finally, we've chosen to make this type FINAL and prevent it from being subtyped further.

It's important to note that BUSINESS_ADDRESS inherits all the attributes and functions associated with its parent class (ADDRESS). Each business address will include attributes for STREET, QUALIFIER, CITY, STATE, ZIP, and INTERNAL_MAIL. The first five are inherited from ADDRESS. The last attribute is unique to BUSINESS_ADDRESS.

This new subtype inherits all the attributes and functions of its parent type.

Once created, BUSINESS_ADDRESS can be used as the data type for columns in tables, much as we did with ADDRESS earlier. It, too, will have constructor, mutator, and observer functions. But more significant is that BUSINESS_ADDRESS instances can substitute for regular ADDRESS instances in tables. We'll discuss this in the next section.

Finally, we should note that some universal DBMSs may support the notion of *multiple inheritance,* much as some object-oriented programming languages do. Briefly, multiple inheritance allows one data type to be derived from multiple data types. For example, we might have data types for HOME and WORK_LOCATION. For employees who strictly work out of their home as part of a telecommuting program, we might create a HOME_OFFICE data type derived from both HOME and WORK_LOCATION.

Some DBMSs even support multiple inheritance (or subtypes based on multiple parents).

Substituting One Type for Another

Subtypes can be substituted for their supertypes.

Inheritance and subtyping often lead to the issue of substituting one type for another. Complex types support this. This means that a column of a table can contain instances of a complex type or any of its subtypes. Doing so provides considerable convenience, simplifying database design and application development.

For example, a magazine publishing firm may wish to maintain a table of its subscribers. For simplicity, we'll assume the table contains two columns: the `NAME` of the subscriber and the `MAIL_ADDRESS` of the subscriber. However, subscribers may be either individuals receiving the magazine at home or businesses receiving it for use in their lobby or corporate library.

This aids database design and application development.

This leads us to the problem of defining a data type for the `MAIL_ADDRESS` column, as we really want to be able to store either `ADDRESS` or `BUSINESS_ADDRESS` instances within this column of each row. By supporting substitution of types within a hierarchy, universal DBMSs can enable us to do so.

For example, we can create a table that stores both regular addresses and business addresses in the same column.

For example, we can create our `SUBSCRIBER` table as shown here, specifying that the `MAIL_ADDRESS` column will have a data type of `ADDRESS`. This permits us to store regular address values or business address values in the table, since business addresses are a subtype of regular addresses. The DBMS will associate a "type tag" with the value of the `MAIL_ADDRESS` column in each row so that it can determine the actual data type.

```
CREATE TABLE SUBSCRIBER
    (NAME            VARCHAR(50),
    MAIL_ADDRESS    ADDRESS)
```

Conceptually, here's what the SUBSCRIBER table might look like after we've inserted some rows. The type tags are internal mechanisms but are shown here in italics for clarity.

SUBSCRIBER

NAME	MAIL_ADDRESS
Jo Ninja	*address type* street: 1509 Tortoise Way . . .
Alley Cats, Inc.	*business_address type* street: 2530 La Mirada Dr. . . .
. . .	. . .

The notion of substituting values of one type for another extends beyond assignments to columns within a table. For example, a subtype can substitute for its supertype in parameter lists passed to functions. This is important, as it facilitates code reuse. For example, a geocoding function that returns *x, y* coordinates for a standard mailing address can also be used with business addresses.

Creating Type "Blueprints"

Each type definition we've discussed so far allows us to create instances of that type. We created an ADDRESS type and stored address values in appropriately defined tables. We did the same thing with BUSINESS_ADDRESS data. Both of these types were defined as *instantiable* at creation.

Sometimes, it's helpful to specify a type "blueprint" for future use.

But some object-oriented programming languages, such as C++, enable users to create new classes of objects that can't be instantiated. These classes (called "abstract" classes in C++) serve as a kind of blueprint for other derived classes. They enable programmers to

This blueprint would serve as a basis for subtypes.

specify a minimal set of attributes and functions associated with the class without actually implementing the class. Implementation is left to those who develop subclasses. But the "blueprint" mandates that somewhere down the line, someone has to implement the functions before instances of that class can be created.

The same concept can be applied in the universal DBMS arena. By specifying a type to be `NOT INSTANTIABLE`, we're preventing users from creating an instance of this type and storing this instance in a table. However, we're enabling others to create subtypes of this type, create and store instances of these subtypes, and implement any necessary functions.

Type Hierarchies and Table Definitions

There are other ways to make use of hierarchies of complex data.

As we learned in Chapter 4, complex data types can be used to define either the column of a table or a table itself. Creating hierarchies of complex types that are used as table definitions gives us the opportunity to create hierarchies of tables, extending certain query capabilities. We'll discuss table hierarchies shortly. First, let's revisit another type definition from Chapter 4.

Recall that we decided to define a complex type for managing information about work projects and later created a table based on this data type. Our complex type, called `PROJECT_TYPE`, contained attributes for the project's ID, code name, description, and budget. Here's our type definition:

```
CREATE TYPE PROJECT_TYPE AS
(ID           INTEGER,
 NAME         VARCHAR(20),
 DESCRIPTION  VARCHAR(50),
 BUDGET       INTEGER)
INSTANTIABLE
NOT FINAL
```

This type definition applies to a broad range of work projects. But perhaps, as time passes, we realize that we need to treat commercial projects somewhat differently. That is, if a given project is expected to produce an item for sale, such as a software application, we may need to adjust our design. Specifically, we might want to add attributes for a release date and a quality assurance rating to commercial projects. (Presumably, other projects, such as research prototypes, do not require such information to be associated with them.)

For example, we can distinguish between regular projects and commercial projects.

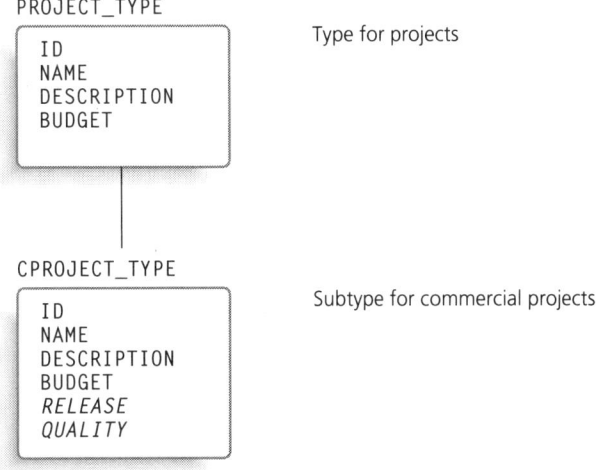

Type for projects

Subtype for commercial projects

For commercial projects, we must track release dates and quality ratings.

The obvious way to achieve our goal is to subtype our PROJECT_TYPE and define a new type specifically for commercial projects. The following SQL statement does so.

Here's how we can create a new subtype for commercial projects.

```
CREATE TYPE CPROJECT_TYPE UNDER PROJECT_TYPE AS
(RELEASE      DATE,
 QUALITY      CHAR(1))
INSTANTIABLE
FINAL
```

The first line creates our new type (CPROJECT_TYPE) as a subtype of PROJECT_TYPE. That is, this type is "under" its parent type in the hierarchy. The next two lines specify the two new attributes associated with commercial projects: a release date and a quality assurance rating. Of course, all the attributes associated with PROJECT_TYPE also apply to instances of CPROJECT_TYPE. Similarly, any functions defined on the parent type will be able to operate on this subtype.

Next, we see that this type is instantiable. If we define a table based on this type, we can insert rows (or instances of this complex type) into the table. Finally, we see that this type is the final element of this hierarchy. In other words, we can't extend or refine this type further by creating additional subtypes underneath it. Enabling type creators to control whether or not subtyping is permitted can help enforce design goals and potentially minimize future maintenance problems.

Managing Table Hierarchies

Tables can also participate in hierarchies.

Hierarchies of data types enable firms to incrementally refine their design, responding to new requirements and reusing existing code in the process. This is another example of how universal DBMSs have adapted object-oriented programming concepts to the database realm. As we've discussed before, a major feature of object-oriented programming languages involves support for hierarchies of object classes.

Doing so offers enhanced data manipulation capabilities.

Table hierarchies are a universal DBMS extension of this concept. But their use is a bit different. The benefits of type hierarchies have largely to do with incremental refinement and code reuse. The primary benefit of table hierarchies is enhanced data manipulation power. With table hierarchies, queries implicitly affect rows involving the referenced table as well as all of its subtables, as we'll see shortly.

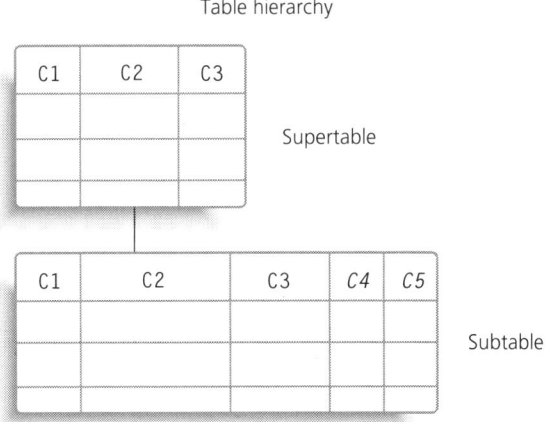

Table hierarchy

Table Hierarchy Example

Since the idea of table hierarchies is a new one, let's explore it further by reviewing an example. Recall the PROJECT table we created earlier based on the PROJECT_TYPE.

Let's consider an example of when this may be useful.

```
CREATE TABLE PROJECT OF PROJECT_TYPE
```

PROJECT

ID	NAME	DESCRIPTION	BUDGET
480	Starburst	Extensible DBMS prototype	10,000,000
...	...	...	...

If desired, we can create a "subtable" for commercial projects. Conceptually, this would be a separate table just like any other, except it would participate in a hierarchy of tables. The following statement creates a CPROJECT table based on the CPROJECT_TYPE. This table will contain rows (or instances of our complex CPROJECT_TYPE) that have attributes for a project's ID, name, description, budget,

Perhaps we'd like to create a subtable for storing data about commercial projects.

This table would be beneath our "parent" project table in a hierarchy.

release date, and quality assurance rating. The CPROJECT table will exist "under" the PROJECT table in a table hierarchy.

```
CREATE TABLE CPROJECT OF CPROJECT_TYPE
UNDER PROJECT
```

CPROJECT

ID	NAME	DESCRIPTION	BUDGET	RELEASE	QUALITY
433	DB2	Universal DBMS	20,000,000	9-17-1997	X
...	...	...	...	...	...

Working with Table Hierarchies

Having done this, queries over the parent table would implicitly affect rows in the subtables.

How data is manipulated through a table hierarchy is more interesting than how the hierarchy itself is created. Queries against the parent table or supertable automatically apply to rows in the subtable(s) as well.

Given the small table hierarchy we've just created for work projects and commercial projects, let's see how some queries might affect them. For purposes of our example, we'll assume additional rows have been added to each table, as shown below.

PROJECT

Here's some sample data for our parent PROJECT table and our CPROJECT subtable.

ID	NAME	DESCRIPTION	BUDGET
480	Starburst	Extensible DBMS prototype	10,000,000
123	R Star	Distributed DBMS	5,000,000
598	System R	RDBMS prototype	2,500,000

CPROJECT

ID	NAME	DESCRIPTION	BUDGET	RELEASE	QUALITY
433	DB2	Universal DBMS	20,000,000	9-17-1997	X
501	DataJoiner	Federated DBMS	5,000,000	11-1-1997	X
706	DB2 Spatial Extender	DBMS Class Library	2,500,000	1-1-1998	Y

Now, let's consider how some queries might affect these tables. We'll start with a data retrieval query. This one requests the names of all projects with a budget exceeding $8 million.

    SELECT NAME
    FROM PROJECT
    WHERE BUDGET > 8,000,000

This query referencing PROJECT would cause a CPROJECT row to be retrieved as well.

The result set would contain two names: Starburst and DB2. Note that Starburst is associated with a row of the PROJECT table, and DB2 is associated with a row of the CPROJECT table. Since the query referenced the PROJECT table, which is a supertable in a hierarchy of tables, the DBMS will automatically search any subtables and retrieve qualifying rows.

A similar situation occurs with data manipulation operations that change the database. For example, attempts to delete rows from the PROJECT table can cause rows in the CPROJECT table to be deleted as well. The following query will cause rows for the System R project, as well DataJoiner and DB2 Spatial Extender projects, to be deleted from the database.

    DELETE FROM PROJECT
    WHERE ID >= 500

The situation is similar for queries involving database update and delete operations.

But new rows are inserted only into the table specified in the query—not other tables in the hierarchy.

However, an insertion of a new row will affect only the table referenced in the INSERT statement. It will not affect any of its subtables in the hierarchy. Thus, the following statement will cause a new row for the POSTGRES project to be inserted into the PROJECT table—and *only* the PROJECT table.

```
INSERT INTO PROJECT VALUES
(507, 'POSTGRES', 'EXTENSIBLE DBMS PROTOTYPE',
8000000)
```

Storing Table Hierarchies

Storage options for hierarchies can vary.

But there's more to table hierarchies than new data manipulation capabilities. Database designers and administrators may have options available to them on how to store these hierarchies. Commercial implementations vary considerably in this area. But there are at least two fundamental options:

Some DBMSs may store all members of a hierarchy as a single table, while others store each member as a separate table.

- Store the entire hierarchy as a single table. Using the previous example, PROJECT and CPROJECT rows would be contained in a single table but would be referenced in queries as though they were in separate tables.

- Store each table in the hierarchy separately, with each table containing the attributes (columns) explicitly defined for it as well as those it may have inherited from its parent table(s). In this case, PROJECT would be stored as one table and CPROJECT as another.

There are trade-offs with each approach.

Note that with the first option, inquiries that span multiple tables in the hierarchy have the potential to be performed more quickly, as rows from different tables could potentially be stored on the same page or at least in close physical proximity to one another. However, it also implies that rows in the "consolidated" table can have different numbers of columns, depending on the data type of each row. For example, rows representing commercial projects will have more attributes than rows representing standard projects. Finally, new indexing extensions may have to be employed, as standard relational DBMS indexes are designed to work with a single table, not a hierarchy of different tables that have been consolidated into one table for storage purposes.

The second option is arguably easier for designers familiar with relational DBMSs to grasp. However, it also means that an inquiry involving instances of a single data type may require accessing multiple tables. For example, the previous query that requested the names of all projects whose budget exceeds $8 million will touch not only the `PROJECT` table but also the `CPROJECT` table, as commercial projects themselves are instances of regular projects.

Using Collections

Another database design option available to administrators of some universal DBMSs involves the use of *collections*. Collections are structures common in some object-oriented programming languages. They provide "containers" for groups of related objects. This same notion is supported by some universal DBMS products, enabling administrators to define table columns that consist of collections of data values. Doing so allows for more complex tabular structures (actually, unnormalized tabular structures) to be defined in a database. But we'll talk more about that later.

Collections are new data types that contain groups of related data values.

First, it's worthwhile to consider the kinds of collections that may be supported by a universal DBMS. Although there's still some debate about these collection types among the SQL standards committee, some vendors already have announced or shipped support for one or more forms of collections. Possible collection types include the following:

They support complex table structures.

Several forms of collections may be supported.

- **Set.** Sets are unordered and contain no duplicate data values.
- **Bag.** Bags are unordered and may contain duplicate data values.
- **List.** Lists are ordered and may contain duplicate values. New values are appended to the end of a list, and the list may grow as long as necessary. There's no predefined boundary or length.
- **Array.** Arrays are ordered and may contain duplicate values. Any element of the array is accessible without starting at the beginning, and new elements can be added anywhere. The extent of an array (that is, its length or boundary) is predefined.

SQL is still used to work with columns that contain collections.

If you're familiar with relational DBMSs, you may be wondering just how these collection types can be accessed. For query purposes, universal DBMSs enable collections to be treated as tables. We'll see examples of this when we explore a few ways in which collections can be used. Such use includes defining tables with multivalue columns and supporting nested table structures.

Defining Tables with Multivalue Columns

Firms can use collections to support multivalue columns. This isn't supported in standard relational DBMS tables.

Collections enable universal DBMSs to store multiple data values within a single column of a row in a table. If you're familiar with traditional relational DBMSs, you know that such products don't support multivalue columns—at least not in a way that the DBMS itself understands. In other words, if you wanted to record the serial number, name, job title, and skill set of each employee, you'd have three broad options with a traditional DBMS:

1. Create two tables, one for EMPLOYEE data and one for SKILL data. The EMPLOYEE table would have columns for the serial number, name, and job title. The SKILL table would have columns for a serial number and skill. With this approach, queries involving employees' names (or job titles) and skills would span

both tables, requiring a *join* to be performed. Unfortunately, joins are typically an expensive operation.

EMPLOYEE

ID	NAME	JOBTITLE
123	C. Ward	Analyst
519	D. Wang	Analyst
480	B. Perez	Engineer
...	...	...

SKILLS

ID	SKILL
519	UNIX
480	C
519	Java
...	...

2. Create a single EMPLOYEE table. This table might have columns for serial number, name, job title, and skills. The skills data would probably be stored as a varying-length character string. The DBMS would not understand that multiple distinct values are actually stored within this column. Thus, writing queries that searched on specific skills would be more complex. Quite possibly, the search logic would be written into applications that read the entire contents of the skills data for appropriate employees to determine if some criteria were met.

EMPLOYEE

ID	NAME	JOBTITLE	SKILLS
123	C. Ward	Analyst	UNIX, NT, TCP/IP
519	D. Wang	Analyst	UNIX, Java
480	B. Perez	Engineer	MVS, SNA, C, COBOL
...	...	...	...

(single character string with no internal structure)

3. Create a single `EMPLOYEE` table with columns for serial number, name, job title, and skill. However, only one skill value would be stored in each row. This would incur considerable data redundancy, as employees with multiple skills would have their serial numbers, names, and job titles stored multiple times.

EMPLOYEE

ID	NAME	JOBTITLE	SKILL
123	C. Ward	Analyst	UNIX
123	C. Ward	Analyst	NT
123	C. Ward	Analyst	TCP/IP
519	D. Wang	Analyst	UNIX
...	...	...	...

Universal DBMSs can offer a fourth choice: store the skills data in a single column defined as some sort of collection data type. In this example, we might choose to store our skills data as a *set* of varying-length character strings. Each string would represent a single skill possessed by the employee in question. The set would contain all of the employee's skills. The use of a set-type collection would mean there's no order associated with these skills, and there are no duplicate skill values allowed.

Here's how we might define a table with a column that contains a set of skills for each employee.

The following example shows how we can create the `EMPLOYEE` table using a set-type collection to store values for the skills of each employee.

```
CREATE TABLE EMPLOYEE
    (ID          EMPLOYEE_ID,
     NAME        VARCHAR(50),
```

```
JOBTITLE   VARCHAR(30),
SKILLS     SET(VARCHAR(20))
)
```

EMPLOYEE

ID	NAME	JOBTITLE	SKILLS
123	C. Ward	Analyst	{UNIX, NT, TCP/IP }
519	D. Wang	Analyst	{UNIX, Java }
480	B. Perez	Engineer	{MVS, SNA, C, COBOL }
...	...	...	...

(set of varying-length character strings)

If you're familiar with SQL, you may be wondering how queries might be supported for structures that contain columns based on collection types. While the specific syntax can vary from product to product, one approach involves treating the collection as a table for purposes of the query. A query to find the names of all employees who have C programming skills might look like this:

And here's how we might query such a table using SQL.

```
SELECT NAME
FROM EMPLOYEE E
WHERE 'C' IN
(SELECT * FROM TABLE (E.SKILLS) S)
```

This query may be easier to read from the bottom up. The last line contains a *subquery*, or a query within a query. If you're familiar with standard SQL in relational environments, you know that subqueries are supported over tables. Here, we're treating the SKILLS column—defined as a set-type collection—as though it were a table for

Note that we treat the set-based column as another table in our query.

purposes of our subquery. This subquery will read all elements of the SKILLS set contained within each row. If a C programming skill is found, the name of the employee will be included in the result returned to the DBMS user.

Building Nested Table Structures

Collections also support nested table structures.

Of course, collections can be based on types other than varying-length character strings, shown in the previous example. Indeed, some products may support collections of any type, including collections of both simple and complex user-defined types. By combining collections with complex types, administrators can define nested table structures—or structures that simulate having rows embedded within the column of a table. In addition, administrators can create tables that contain sets of references to rows in other tables. We'll discuss both possibilities here.

Complex types are combined with collections to achieve this.

Let's consider an example. This time, we'll define a complex type to represent employees and call this new type EMP_TYPE. Associated with each employee will be an ID, name, job title, reference to a manager, and a set of projects the employee is working on. We'll then create a new EMPLOYEE table based on this type.

```
CREATE TYPE EMP_TYPE AS
(ID           INTEGER,
NAME          VARCHAR(50),
JOBTITLE      VARCHAR(30),
MANAGER       REF(EMP_TYPE),
ASSIGNMENT    SET(PROJECT_TYPE)
)
INSTANTIABLE
NOT FINAL
```

Again, we'll step through this type definition. The first line specifies that we're creating a type called EMP_TYPE. This complex type contains attributes based on three simple, built-in data types: ID, an integer; NAME, a varying-length character string; and JOBTITLE, a varying-length character string. Next, we represent the employee's manager by defining a reference to an instance of the employee type. This is one way in which we can model the *m:1* relationship between employees and their managers in our database.

Here, employee data can contain references to rows of multiple projects for each employee.

The last attribute is what enables us to use this type to define a complex table structure in which sets of information about projects are nested within the ASSIGNMENT column of the EMPLOYEE table. This supports situations in which a single employee is working on multiple projects. As you may recall, PROJECT_TYPE was a complex type we originally defined in Chapter 4 and revisited again earlier in this chapter.

Having completed our new EMP_TYPE definition, we can now create a new EMPLOYEE table based on this row type. Conceptually, the EMPLOYEE table will support nesting of rows within one of its columns (ASSIGNMENT). More accurately, it will contain a set of project data within one column of each row.

We use this type to define a table, creating a nested structure in the process.

```
CREATE TABLE EMPLOYEE OF EMP_TYPE
    (SCOPE FOR MANAGER IS EMPLOYEE)
```

But perhaps we'd prefer to have data related to projects exist in a separate table rather than be directly included in our EMPLOYEE table. From a traditional database design perspective, this makes more sense and has the added advantage of minimizing data redundancy. In this case, we can define our ASSIGNMENT column to contain a set of references to PROJECT_TYPE instances. Presumably, these instances exist in a separate table, such as the PROJECT table we defined earlier.

Alternatively, we can combine collections and references to complex types to model data relationships in a different way.

```
CREATE TYPE EMP_TYPE AS
(ID           INTEGER,
NAME          VARCHAR(50),
JOBTITLE      VARCHAR(30),
MANAGER       REF(EMP_TYPE),
ASSIGNMENT    SET(REF(PROJECT_TYPE))
)
INSTANTIABLE
NOT FINAL
```

If we created an `EMPLOYEE` table based on this new `EMP_TYPE` definition, we'd have an `ASSIGNMENT` column capable of containing multiple references to various projects. This is another way of representing the fact that a single employee can work on multiple projects.

As you might imagine, we could extend our database design to model *m:n* relationships by using complex types that contain collections of references to other rows based on complex types. For example, we could have revised our database design to enable each `PROJECT_TYPE` instance to contain an additional attribute referencing a set of `EMP_TYPE`s. Then the corresponding `PROJECT` table would capture the set of employees working on each project. Such a design reflects the fact that employees may work on multiple projects, and projects may be staffed by multiple employees.

Combining Complex Types, Collections, and Hierarchies

A single database design can make use of multiple types, collections, and hierarchies.

We've covered a lot of material so far. By now, you've been exposed to a variety of forms of user-defined data types and how these types can be used in hierarchies. You've also seen how tables themselves can be arranged in hierarchies, and how tables can be created that possess more complex or unusual structures than are possible in a traditional relational DBMS.

But our examples so far have largely treated each of these topics separately, mainly to keep discussions as simple as possible. However, it would be misleading to imply that universal DBMSs require administrators and designers to approach these topics independently. Indeed, simple and complex user-defined types, built-in data types, collections, and hierarchies may be used together if desired.

We won't explore the full range of possibilities here. Such a discussion would be considerable and is beyond the scope of this introductory book. Instead, we'll just review one example that ties together some of the concepts introduced earlier throughout this text.

We'll just take one simple example to illustrate that point.

The following example revisits our `EMP_TYPE`. In this latest incarnation of employees, we define a complex data type that makes use of several universal DBMS mechanisms: built-in data types, a simple (distinct) user-defined type, a complex data type, collection types, and references to complex data types.

Here's another way to model employees that perhaps captures more real-world complexity than earlier examples.

```
CREATE TYPE EMP_TYPE AS
(ID          EMPLOYEE_ID,
 NAME        VARCHAR(50),
 HOME        ADDRESS,
 JOBTITLE    VARCHAR(30),
 APPRAISAL   INTEGER,
 SKILLS      LIST(VARCHAR(20)),
 MANAGER     REF(EMP_TYPE),
 ASSIGNMENT  SET(REF(PROJECT_TYPE) )
)
INSTANTIABLE
NOT FINAL
```

In this case, the `ID` attribute is based on a user-defined distinct type (`EMPLOYEE_ID`) we created in Chapter 3. The `NAME`, `JOBTITLE`, and `APPRAISAL` attributes are based on system-supplied (or built-in) data types. The HOME attribute is based on a user-defined complex data type (ADDRESS) that we created in Chapter 4 and discussed again earlier in this chapter. The SKILLS attribute is a list-type collection of skills possessed by the employee, perhaps arranged in order of experience. In this case, the collection contains varying-length character strings. The MANAGER attribute is a reference to another instance of EMP_TYPE, or another employee. And the ASSIGNMENT attribute is a set of references to PROJECT_TYPE instances, or a set of projects the employee is working on.

Having created this type, we can define a table to contain instances of this type. If desired, we can create additional subtypes of our EMP_TYPE, as well as additional subtables of our EMPLOYEE table.

Managing Type Creation

We've seen how new data types can be created and used in a universal DBMS environment. As you can imagine, it takes some skill to determine which new data types should be created and how these data types should be worked into the design of a database.

Deciding what types should be created and when they should be used takes skill. It's best to restrict this activity to administrators or designers.

In general, it's best to make type creation the responsibility of a database designer or database administrator. Such individuals typically have a good understanding of the data they need to manage as well as the types of applications that will be working with this data. This knowledge is important, as an administrator will need to not only define new data types but also decide how (and when) these data types are to be used during subsequent creation of tables.

As with relational DBMSs, universal DBMSs require that each column of a table be defined on a specific type. And although universal DBMSs are more flexible than their traditional counterparts—supporting type substitution within a hierarchy, for example—there are limits to this flexibility.

Once a column has been defined to be of a specific data type, its type cannot be altered. (The same is true for relational DBMSs.) Thus, the HOME column of our EMPLOYEE table cannot be altered from an ADDRESS type to a varying-length character string, or vice versa. The only way to accomplish such a task would be to drop the EMPLOYEE table and re-create it with a new type definition for the column. Of course, dropping the table means its rows will be deleted, and we will have to reload them. If the table is big, this can be a time-consuming task.

Therefore, it's important not to take database design lightly. User-defined types offer firms considerable power and flexibility; they also contribute to data integrity. And although they're relatively easy to create (as we've already seen), their implications are not trivial. Certainly for the early stages of a project, it's wise to confine type creation to a small number of people. Some universal DBMSs make this relatively easy to do by establishing data type creation as a new security privilege that must be granted to specific individuals or groups of users.

Some DBMSs introduce new security privileges for type creation and type usage.

Summary

Universal DBMSs introduce new design options. In earlier chapters, we saw how firms can create their own simple and complex data types. Here, we've explored how complex types can participate in type hierarchies, with subtypes inheriting the attributes (and ability to support any user-defined functions) associated with their parent types or supertypes. These type hierarchies are another way in which universal DBMSs have applied object-oriented programming concepts to the database arena.

Universal DBMSs may support a number of features that introduce new database design options.

Collections and hierarchies are two of them. They enable firms to define unusual or complex table structures.

Such support reflects an adoption of certain object-oriented concepts.

Type collections—or groups of related objects—are also supported in certain object-oriented programming languages and have been implemented in some universal DBMSs. Administrators can create unusual and more complex table structures using various kinds of collections but still query values contained within those collections via SQL. And finally, some universal DBMSs support table hierarchies and extend the scope of function supported by SQL data manipulation operations that work with such tables.

To be sure, this wide range of options gives administrators more to think about. Potential benefits associated with the capabilities discussed in this chapter include

- new data modeling options designed to help firms cope with complex real-world structures and relationships among elements of these structures
- greater support for object-oriented programming concepts, which can lessen the work required to effectively map object-oriented class structures into a DBMS environment
- greater support for code reuse
- potential for reduced maintenance

CHAPTER 7

Providing Quick Access to Custom Data

In this chapter, we'll explore ways in which universal DBMSs try to ensure reasonable performance.

While universal DBMSs provide a flexible, extensible environment for their users, these characteristics aren't terribly useful if the system doesn't perform well. To ensure reasonable performance, some universal DBMS vendors have extended traditional indexing and optimization support to accommodate new user requirements. Although such enhancements are beyond the scope of SQL standards efforts, they are nonetheless important in commercial environments. These efforts focus on ways to improve access to the variety of data managed by and stored within the DBMS itself.

In this chapter, we'll talk about some of the features that can significantly affect universal DBMS performance, drawing on examples from commercial products when appropriate. As you might expect, support for such enhancements varies considerably from product to product. But we'll try to cover the broad range of alternatives that vendors, such as IBM, Informix, and Oracle, are known to be working on or already support as of this writing.

It's worth noting, however, that universal DBMSs are still relatively new commercial offerings. Early development efforts have tended to focus on supporting new functions (such as an extensible type system) rather than tuning existing capabilities. As universal DBMSs become more widely used, we can expect to see more emphasis placed on performance tuning features.

Indexing

Indexing enhancements can be a key factor.

Indexes are commonly used by relational DBMSs to speed searches of certain queries. They offer an alternative to sequentially scanning each page of the table, helping the DBMS to more quickly pinpoint rows that satisfy a user request. In some respects, they're similar to the index of a book: both contain key values and references to the locations of these key values, and both help avoid the need to inspect each page for the desired information.

Index Structure in a Relational DBMS

Relational DBMSs typically use a B+-tree index structure.

Relational DBMSs use B+-tree index structures (or a close derivative) to maintain information about the data values of one or more columns in the rows of a table. For each key value entry in the index, the location of its row is also stored, usually in the format of a row identifier (RID) that can be mapped to an area within a data page.

B+-tree indexes are multilevel structures useful for speeding a variety of queries typical to business applications that work with traditional data types. Consider the following query, seeking the names of all employees who have job codes 7 through 9.

```
EMPLOYEE TABLE
   ID, NAME, JOBCODE, SALARY, . . .

SELECT NAME
FROM EMPLOYEE
WHERE JOBCODE BETWEEN 7 AND 9
```

One way the DBMS can resolve this query is to scan through each data page of the table, checking the JOBCODE value for each row to see if it equals 7, 8, or 9. However, if an index was defined on the JOBCODE column, its use is likely to speed the search, particularly if the table is large and a relatively small percentage of the rows have JOBCODE values that meet the specified conditions. Improved search speed is largely due to a reduction in I/O processing when compared with a full scan of the table.

Such indexes often speed searches of range queries involving common forms of business data.

To understand how this works, we'll need to briefly discuss B+-tree indexes. Such indexes contain a single root page. On this page are pointers to subsequent pages at the next branch or level of the tree, as well as the highest key value associated with each of these pages. The lowest pages in the tree, called the *leaf pages,* contain key values for each row in the table, as well as the corresponding locations (RIDs) of these key values.

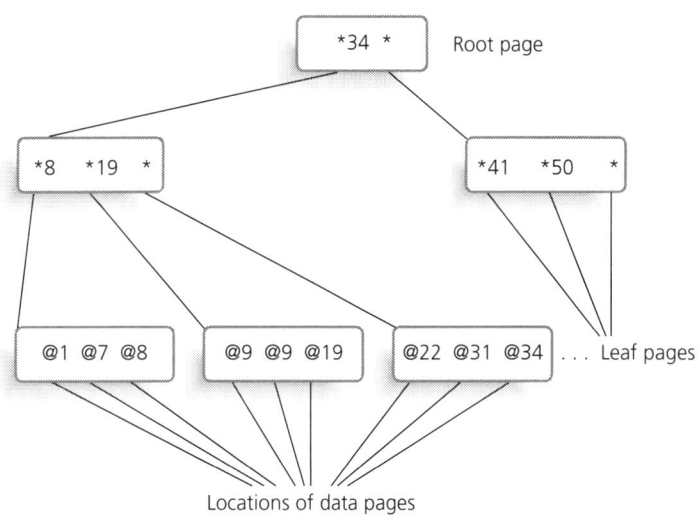

Here's a sample B+-tree architecture. Leaf pages contain key values for indexed columns and the locations of their corresponding rows.

The DBMS knows how to traverse this structure quickly to pinpoint needed information.

The previous figure depicts a sample three-level B+-tree index structure. Assume this was the index defined on the JOBCODE column of the EMPLOYEE table. To resolve the user's request for names of employees who have job codes of 7 through 9, the DBMS could use this index. To do so, it would start at the root page and find that the left branch contains key values of 34 or less. It would proceed down this branch and determine that two index pages contain values within this key range (the leftmost branch contains values of 8 or less, and the next branch on the left contains values of 9 through 19). Ultimately, pages on both of these branches would be read for the appropriate key values. Once located in the index, these values would yield the RIDs or locations of corresponding rows.

Often, such indexes reduce I/O processing.

Thus, B+-tree indexes can reduce the I/O processing associated with resolving certain queries by enabling the DBMS to more quickly pinpoint the location of the desired data without having to scan through each data page.

In addition to B+-tree indexes, a number of DBMSs support hash access to data or bitmap indexing. Like B+-trees, these access methods were built by the DBMS vendor directly into the product to speed access for certain types of operations. For example, hashing performs well for queries searching for an exact match on some particular key value. Bitmap indexes are frequently used to speed multi-dimensional searches typical of online analytical processing (OLAP) applications.

But these techniques—B+-tree indexes, hash access, and bitmap indexes—were designed to speed searches of queries involving traditional data types (primarily character strings and numbers). Since universal DBMSs seek to support new types of applications and allow firms to define new data types and functions to the system, new indexing enhancements need to be considered.

New Index Structures for New Data Types

One reason why universal DBMSs have an extensible data type system is that it's unrealistic to depend on a single DBMS vendor to build native support for all possible data types into its product. A similar argument can be made in favor of user-defined access methods. It's unrealistic to expect any one vendor to deliver all desired access methods to speed a wide range of searches involving all possible forms of data.

But universal DBMSs need index structures that are extensible.

To be sure, defining new access methods requires considerable time and skill—perhaps more than most firms are willing to dedicate to such activity. However, even if your organization doesn't anticipate a need to be able to integrate new index structures into a universal DBMS, it's important to look for products that support this ability. Why?

A number of third-party vendors are building class libraries for universal DBMSs. These class libraries introduce new data types and functions. To ensure they perform reasonably well, vendors who sell such libraries often need to use access methods other than traditional B+-tree indexes (or full table scans). Since the success of their products depends, in part, on acceptable performance levels, some of these vendors are willing to make the engineering investment necessary to be able to introduce new access methods into a universal DBMS environment.

New indexing technology can be quite important to those who build class libraries to support new applications.

There are at least three approaches to solving the problem of how to associate new access methods with a universal DBMS:

Indexing can be enhanced in three general ways.

- Allow external access methods to be loosely integrated within a universal DBMS environment.

- Allow existing DBMS access methods to be extended as desired.
- Allow entirely new access methods to be defined to the DBMS.

We'll explore each in this chapter.

Of course, these approaches aren't mutually exclusive. A universal DBMS could support all three. But implementing new access methods with any of these approaches does require a reasonable level of design and programming skills, as well as some domain-specific knowledge. For this reason, each of these approaches tends to be targeted at independent software vendors rather than IT organizations. Nonetheless, it's certainly possible for an IT group to undertake this effort, if desired.

Maintaining External Indexes

One option involves introducing new access methods outside the DBMS.

The first option—enabling firms to build access methods outside the DBMS—offers two primary advantages. To the DBMS vendor, it's arguably the easiest approach to take, requiring relatively modest changes to be made to the engine when compared with other alternatives. To a third-party vendor (such as one building a class library), it offers a means to apply custom index technology to a broader environment without major effort.

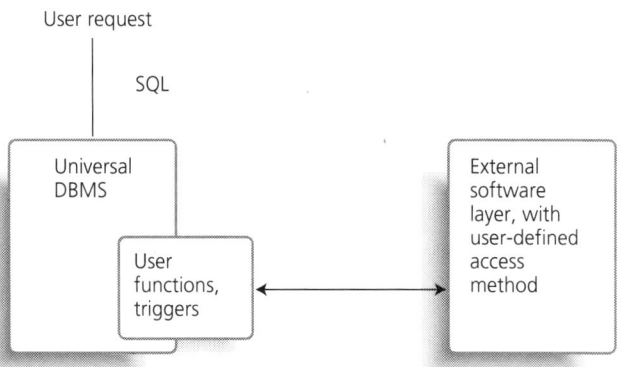

Here's what such an architecture might look like. Functions and triggers help keep the external index in sync with database changes.

As you are probably aware, a number of vendors have long employed specialized indexing technologies to satisfy specific applications. For example, text retrieval systems often use inverted lists or other mechanisms to speed queries for full-text documents. Some of these access methods are highly tuned, employing proprietary technologies to achieve a competitive advantage in the market. Their use is integral to other functions supported by the product or application. But reimplementing these technologies *inside* a universal DBMS may be undesirable for several reasons:

■ It can be expensive to do.

■ The process of modifying native DBMS index support varies from product to product. To cover the broadest market, an independent vendor would have to undertake the same development effort multiple times—an unattractive proposition.

■ It's likely to expose proprietary technology to other vendors or the public, at least to some degree.

Some third-party vendors favor this approach for business reasons.

So, maintaining external access methods and coupling these somehow with a universal DBMS can be more appealing to independent software vendors. But what's in it for the users of these universal DBMSs? Presumably, it might motivate established vendors with advanced, proven technology to couple their software with universal DBMSs, enabling DBMS users to leverage these technologies in some way.

This approach can help bring new technologies into the broad universal DBMS environment.

It should be noted, however, that maintaining external indexes is an approach that trades off development costs for maximum performance gains, at least to some degree. Clearly, it requires less effort to loosely couple an external access method to the DBMS than to redefine (and re-create) the access method inside the DBMS itself. In some situations, a "lightweight" approach to supporting new access methods may be the only viable alternative. And maintaining an

But there's clearly a trade-off.

external index that's capable of speeding up certain searches is better than doing nothing at all.

Performance gains are clearly possible. But a built-in access method offers greater performance potential than an external one.

But this approach is not without drawbacks. The greatest opportunities for performance gains can be achieved by extending existing DBMS access methods or introducing entirely new access methods into the DBMS itself. We'll talk about each of these alternatives shortly. First, let's consider some of the potential limitations with maintaining external indexes.

Because the new index structure or other access method exists outside of the DBMS, data can't always be filtered as close to the source. Instead, at least some data filtering will be handled by the external access method based upon data supplied to it by the DBMS. In some cases, the DBMS will have to pass along all rows that *may* qualify, potentially causing many rows to be read from disk that will later be discarded because they don't match some user-specified search criteria.

Presumably, the new access method will still introduce new technology that can help speed the search or support advanced capabilities. An example of the latter might involve a user request (specified in SQL) to retrieve the publication titles and order numbers of all documents that contain the words "universal DBMS" and "research" in the same sentence. Text retrieval systems typically have implemented access methods that can quickly conduct proximity-based searches of word phrases. Again, an external index is one way of enabling a universal DBMS to capitalize on such features.

But maintaining an external index does introduce some overhead and complexity into the environment. Code has to be developed to ensure that data in the external index is kept in sync with the database tables, which may be modified by users at any time. Triggers and event alerters, discussed in Chapter 5, can help here. But they can also add greater overhead to the DBMS environment, increasing the work performed for any transaction that inserts, updates, or deletes data associated with an external index. And they weren't designed to enforce external data integrity and concurrency control issues.

And something must be done to ensure the external index remains in sync with the database as changes are made or utilities are run.

Finally, the impact of common database utility operations has to be considered when external indexes are used. For example, how will database backup and recovery operations be coordinated with this external component? How will the external index be modified when a LOAD operation is performed to add a large amount of data to the table? What will happen to the index when a database reorganization occurs, causing data from one page to be moved to another?

Universal DBMS vendors can take various approaches to enabling external access methods to be associated with their products. For example, user-defined functions (discussed in an earlier chapter) can be written to call external software, such as a text retrieval engine, passing it relevant parameters that reflect the user's SQL request. This software would retrieve any additional data needed from the universal DBMS, perform the search using its own access methods, and return a result (or result set) to the user-defined function. The function could take additional action (if needed) or simply pass these results directly back to the SQL user.

Extending Existing Index Structures

Another option involves extending existing B+-tree structures to support user-defined types.

Some universal DBMSs enable users and third parties to enhance their native DBMS index structures. Such enhancements can involve enabling a standard B+-tree index to work with user-defined types and layering new indexing structures on top of an existing B+-tree structure. We'll discuss both of these options.

As we mentioned earlier, relational DBMSs support B+-tree structures that can index key values for columns defined on built-in data types. These data types are typically various forms of character strings and numbers. But universal DBMSs enable users to define new types to the system. It may be desirable to enable administrators to create B+-tree indexes for columns based on these new types. Some universal DBMSs support this, offering potential performance gains for queries that specify search criteria (or query predicates) involving user-defined types.

Some extensions allow for new access methods to be built upon the B+-tree.

Some products also enable new access methods to be "grafted" onto the native B+-tree structure. We'll discuss a real-world example of when this approach can be useful.

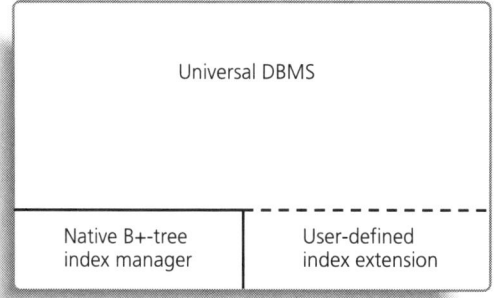

Consider the challenges of extending a DBMS environment to support the types of geographic requests we discussed in earlier chapters. An example of a geographic request involved determining all the Italian restaurants within a 1-mile walking distance of a hotel. Here, the location of Italian restaurants serves as a filtering mechanism for a query.

Specialized applications often require specialized access methods.

B+-tree structures are often used in relational DBMS environments to quickly pinpoint qualifying rows in a table. However, B+-tree structures are designed to work with one-dimensional data: an employee ID, a salary, a job code, or similar types of data. But geographic data is inherently multidimensional, containing 2D or 3D properties to represent the location of an object in space. In 2D space, objects are usually represented by x, y coordinates; in 3D space, objects are represented by x, y, z coordinates.

Consider the area of geographic analysis.

For this reason (and others), researchers and vendors have explored a number of other access methods to speed searches involving geographic data. Many such alternatives have been developed, including R-trees, quad trees, grid files, and K-D-B trees. Some of these have been implemented in commercial Geographic Information Systems (GIS) for years.

Technologies other than B+-trees have been used for years.

One leading GIS vendor makes use of grid files to speed spatial searches. Very briefly, this structure calls for logically imposing a grid over objects in geographic space, recording information about which objects reside in all or part of each cell in the grid. Conducting a spatial search involves (1) determining which cell(s) correspond to the user's search criteria, and (2) using the grid file to identify objects within the appropriate cell(s). Once these objects are identified, additional filtering can be done if necessary.

Here's one way in which B+-tree indexes can be extended to support a new access method for geographic data.

This GIS vendor collaborated with a universal DBMS vendor to graft grid file technology onto an existing B+-tree structure. Doing so was possible because the DBMS vendor supports user-defined index extensions. An abbreviated example of one way in which such an extension can be defined to IBM's DB2 Universal Database appears below.

```
CREATE INDEX EXTENSION GRIDS
(LEVELS VARCHAR(20))
WITH INDEX KEYS FOR (S SHAPE)
TRANSFORMED BY GRIDENTRY
    (S..MBR..XMIN, S..MBR..YMIN,
    S..MBR..XMAX, S..MBR..YMAX)
WITH SEARCH METHODS FOR KEYS
    (GX, GY, X1, Y1, X2, Y2)
WHEN WITHIN (R SHAPE) . . .
WHEN OVERLAP (R SHAPE) . . .
WHEN CONTAINS (R SHAPE) . . .
```

Some of these statements are peculiar to one means of implementing a grid file structure, so we won't cover them in detail. Rather, we'll focus on the fundamental process for defining an index extension, using the previous example as a reference point.

In this case, an index extension is defined using SQL. The extension is capable of supporting a multilevel grid structure for indexing values of type SHAPE. A SHAPE is a user-defined complex data type, containing a number of attributes not shown here. A transformation function called GRIDENTRY is identified that will work with shape values, calculating the minimum bounding rectangle (MBR) that will enclose the indexed shape. The final statements identify new methods for searching through this grid file structure to resolve spatial queries involving user-defined functions that help determine relationships among spatial objects (for example, if a point is located within a polygon or if one region overlaps another). When each of these user-defined functions was created, some SQL clauses were added to specify that this user-defined index extension can be used to resolve queries involving the function.

Now that you have some idea of what index extensions mean, let's consider the relative advantages and disadvantages of this approach. Here, new code is introduced within the DBMS engine environment to alter (or enhance) existing access methods in new ways. This provides for tighter integration than an external access method, offering potential for greater performance benefits. In addition, some of the possible maintenance problems associated with external indexes disappear because the DBMS is made aware of the new indexing technology and can manage the index directly.

This approach provides for tighter integration—and potentially better performance—than building an external access method.

However, this approach often requires more skill from the individual(s) implementing the new access method. At the very least, it requires the implementer to develop a solid working knowledge of the target DBMS. Debugging can be a challenge but must be carefully done to avoid compromising the DBMS in any way. And if different universal DBMS offerings must be supported, design and coding changes are likely to be required for each target platform.

But it does take some work to build.

Introducing Completely New Index Structures

A final alternative—and arguably the most aggressive—is to enable third parties to introduce entirely new index structures to the DBMS. These indexes structures would exist independent of native B+-tree structures rather than being an enhancement upon them.

Alternatively, a DBMS might enable firms to introduce entirely new access methods into the DBMS itself.

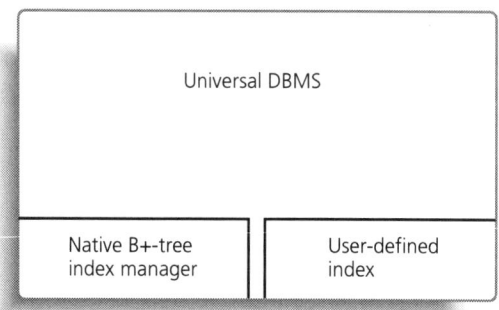

This provides an even greater level of DBMS integration.

The goal of this approach is much the same as that of the extended B+-tree approach: to improve performance for certain searches, often when those searches involve custom data types. Both approaches attempt to achieve this by introducing new indexing technology into the DBMS itself. The difference involves the level at which the integration of this user-defined indexing technology occurs.

Because index extensions are layered on top of an existing B+-tree structure, the very lowest levels of the DBMS engine can remain unchanged. That is, certain internal DBMS components perceive the "new" index to be the same as the native index. This reduces the work involved for the DBMS vendor and (potentially) for the index implementer.

Nonetheless, the ability to introduce a brand-new access method to the DBMS provides for a greater level of flexibility than is possible with an extension approach. In certain cases, it may also yield performance benefits, as B+-tree structures aren't ideal for all situations.

But the development process is far from trivial.

When compared with external access methods, new built-in access methods offer potential for greater performance gains. Presumably, code to keep the new index in sync with the table on which it was defined will be a part of the access method creation process. Thus, triggers and event alerters aren't needed to do this (again eliminating some overhead when the system is deployed in production).

Furthermore, the access method creation process should involve coding any necessary extensions to DBMS utilities to ensure the integrity of the index isn't compromised when typical administrative functions are performed. For example, backup and recovery operations must include not only relevant tables but all indexes defined on these tables—whether the indexes are native structures supported by the DBMS vendor or new structures introduced by someone else. Finally, the implementation must be tested thoroughly.

Indexing User-Defined Functions

In addition to enabling firms to introduce new or enhanced access methods, some universal DBMSs enable firms to define indexes on the output of a user-defined function. This provides for additional flexibility and offers potential performance gains in certain situations.

In a relational DBMS environment, indexes are created on one or more columns of a table. As we discussed earlier in this chapter, the index contains key values for the column(s) on which it was defined as well as the locations of rows containing these values. Thus, relational DBMS indexes are designed to track values of data stored in a table.

But in a universal DBMS environment, it's sometimes useful to be able to create indexes on user-defined functions—particularly if the functions are frequently used as search conditions in queries. For example, if an interior designer often wants to see images and pricing information for fabrics with a high content of blue color, a programmer may have developed a function to ascertain the degree of "blue" found in images associated with a FABRIC table. Presumably, this

Finally, some universal DBMSs can index the output of a user-defined function rather than key values of columns.

Often, a modified B+-tree structure is used.

function would return a numeric value that indicates if a high or low level of this color exists for a given image.

In this case, performance may be improved if an index is created on the output of the user-defined function. It might even be wise to store this information in a B+-tree structure. Doing so implies that when new rows are added to the table, the user-defined function would be run in order to compute the output and store this in the index, along with the location (RID) of the row. Updates to data that is the target of user-defined functions would also require computation in order to keep the index entries accurate. And, of course, deleting existing rows would cause corresponding index entries to be deleted.

Some universal DBMSs offer enhanced B+-tree implementations that can support indexing of user-defined functions. Creating such indexes is similar to the standard index creation process of a relational DBMS. But instead of specifying one or more columns to be the target of the index creation, an administrator specifies a user-defined function to be applied to data values of one or more columns.

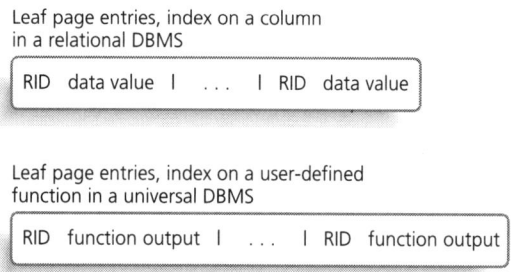

Here's how a portion of such an index might look when compared with a typical relational DBMS index.

The following example shows the syntax supported by one universal DBMS vendor (Informix) to enable administrators to create an index on a user-defined function. In this case, the `COLOR_INDEX` is defined for the `FABRICS` table. The index will employ a B+-tree structure with key values based on the output of the user-defined `BLUE` function, as applied to the `IMAGE` column of the table.

And here's an example of how an index on a user-defined function might be created.

```
FABRICS TABLE
   ID, PRICE, MANUFACTURER, IMAGE

CREATE INDEX COLOR_INDEX
ON FABRICS
USING B-TREE (BLUE(IMAGE))
```

It's worth noting, however, that such index extensions are most useful for certain types of functions—particularly functions that return a scalar (or single) value. Other kinds of functions containing complex expressions that are tested against a Boolean value typically won't benefit from defining an index on the function's output. However, those functions may benefit from other forms of user-defined indexing, discussed earlier.

Optimization

New or enhanced access methods represent one way by which performance can potentially be improved in a universal DBMS environment. However, optimization technology is also quite important. Some vendors provide mechanisms to enable users to influence decisions made by the optimizer regarding data access strategies.

Optimization issues are also important.

As we discussed in Chapter 1, relational DBMSs differed sharply from their predecessors by enabling users to specify *what* data they wanted to access, not *how* that data was to be accessed. The DBMS component critical to making this possible is the optimizer.

Optimizers determine how data is to be accessed.

The optimizer is responsible for evaluating different ways of accessing the data necessary to satisfy a user's request. Alternatives may include scanning each page of the table, using a single index, or (perhaps) using multiple indexes.

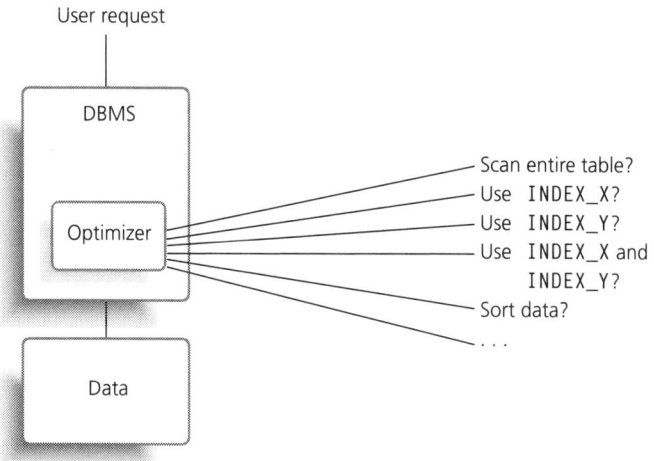

They consider many options, including use of index(es) and table scans.

They consult catalog statistics to estimate the costs of different options and select a "cheap" one.

To assess various data strategies, optimizers estimate a cost for each viable alternative. A variety of statistical information is used to calculate these estimates. Such statistical information is stored in the *system catalog,* which is a set of tables used by the DBMS for various purposes. Examples of catalog data of interest to the optimizer include the existence of indexes for a table, the number of pages in a table, and information about the distribution of data values for indexed columns. The latter is particularly relevant if data is skewed such that occurrences of specific values are rather frequent and occurrences of other values are relatively rare.

What does all this have to do with universal DBMSs? Like standard relational DBMSs, universal systems include an optimizer responsible for determining an efficient access strategy for satisfying the user's query. And, just like in a relational DBMS environment, the "intelligence" of the optimizer can impact system performance. A poor optimizer might select an inefficient way of retrieving desired data, resulting in unnecessary I/O, sorts, or CPU consumption.

This optimization task becomes more complex in a universal DBMS.

But universal DBMS optimizers must cope with situations that are hard to anticipate. After all, users can define new types, new functions, and new access methods to the DBMS. Making smart data access decisions under such circumstances can be quite challenging.

For this reason, some DBMS vendors enable firms to influence optimization decisions or "educate" the optimizer in some way. Let's take a look at some general approaches to coping with this situation.

Some products enable firms to "educate" or influence their optimizers when working with new types and functions.

Providing Optimization Hints or Instructions

One technique calls for programmers or users to include data access instructions in their applications or queries. Presumably, the user is aware of the access alternatives available, understands the scope of work the query will generate, and is more capable of identifying an efficient data access strategy than the optimizer would be able to do on its own. Such a scenario is certainly possible in a universal DBMS environment, and allowing this type of user to "guide" the optimizer can be an important performance tuning mechanism.

One approach involves writing hints or data access directives.

At least one DBMS vendor (Oracle) supports this approach by allowing users to embed a data access "hint" directly within an SQL statement. In this case, the DBMS will detect the user's directive and avoid assessing other options (and estimating associated costs with each). Instead, it will simply employ the data access strategy specified by the user. If the access strategy is invalid, the DBMS will automatically optimize the query and select a valid strategy of its own. A strategy might be invalid if a user specified a nonexistent index.

If the supplied hint is good, performance may improve.

This approach to influencing optimization strategies is relatively straightforward and simple to code, making use of SQL. It offers firms a direct means of influencing the selected access strategy. Assuming such instructions are coded by knowledgeable users, it's possible that performance will improve because a better data access strategy will be employed.

But bad hints can cause performance to suffer. And firms may need to reconsider their hints as the database design changes or new releases of the DBMS are installed.

However, this approach is not without its drawbacks. Hard-coding data access instructions in an application or a query forces a programmer or user to become more aware of optimization issues than he or she might like to be. If the programmer makes an honest mistake or has limited skill, the directive could cause the optimizer to select a poorer access strategy than if it had been left to its own devices. A third consideration is that optimization instructions prevent the DBMS from taking advantage of database design changes (such as the addition of an index) that could potentially improve performance. Finally, if multiple applications or queries involve DBMS operations that require "helping" the optimizer select an efficient access strategy, appropriate instructions will have to be coded into *each* of these.

Judicious use is probably best.

Nonetheless, giving firms the option of supplying optimization hints or instructions can be useful under certain circumstances. Like many other features, data access directives are best when used judiciously and after some testing has been done to ensure they will achieve the desired effect.

Influencing Cost Estimation

Another means of enhancing query optimization involves enabling users to influence the cost estimation associated with various data access strategies. Relational DBMS optimizers estimate the costs associated with various operations by computing the anticipated CPU resource use and estimated I/O processing required. If current statistics are available, these contribute to such estimates. For some operations (particularly those for which applicable statistics are not available or not collected), the DBMS factors some default assumptions into its cost estimation.

When new data types and new index structures are introduced into a universal DBMS, it can be difficult to accurately estimate costs associated with data access strategies that could be employed for a given query. Some vendors enable firms to influence the cost estimate by supplying the optimizer with an "adjustment factor" that can augment the default cost assumptions that would otherwise be used.

In addition, some universal DBMSs enable users to educate the optimizer on the estimated costs associated with executing various user-defined functions. In traditional DBMS environments, such capability is unnecessary. The DBMS is shipped with a predefined set of supported SQL functions, and the optimizer has been programmed (by the DBMS vendor) to understand relative costs of executing these functions.

But as user-defined functions are added to a universal DBMS, the optimizer has no way of accurately estimating execution costs unless some additional mechanism is provided. Allowing the optimizer to arbitrarily associate a cost with a new function is likely to result in performance that is far from ideal in many cases.

Some products provide various techniques to influence the cost estimates calculated for different access options.

A user-defined "adjustment factor" is one technique.

A second optimization extension involves cost estimates for user-defined functions.

For this reason, some universal DBMSs enable programmers to specify the estimated costs of executing functions they have defined. As you might imagine, the mechanisms for doing so vary from product to product. One approach, for example, calls for users to update a system catalog table to include statistical estimates for various costs associated with function execution. Such costs may include the estimated number of I/Os per invocation of the function and the estimated number of instructions per invocation of the function. Another approach involves specifying routines or other information that can influence optimization as part of the function declaration.

A third affects efficient transformation of queries.

Finally, some universal DBMSs enable firms to include other information in their definitions of user-defined functions that can assist with optimization. A simple example here involves specifying a "negator" for a function. As it turns out, processing queries that specify negation ("Show me the employees who do not earn more than $50,000 a year") can be expensive to perform because they inhibit the use of available indexes. For this reason, relational DBMSs transform such queries (when possible) into logical equivalents that can be processed more efficiently. The previous example could be transformed into "Show me the employees who earn less than or equal to $50,000 a year."

Again, it may not be possible for the DBMS to transform user-defined functions in such a manner, as the DBMS wouldn't know the appropriate negator function. Some universal DBMSs enable programmers to specify negator functions (as well as similar functions useful for optimization) when creating their own SQL functions.

Summary

Since performance is critical in many IT environments, universal DBMSs often provide multiple features to influence overall system performance. The issue is a particularly challenging one, as the extensibility of a universal DBMS means that indexing and optimization techniques have to be more flexible than those traditionally present in standard relational DBMSs.

Performance issues can become complex in universal DBMSs.

We've discussed various approaches to ensuring reasonable performance in an environment where firms may introduce new data types and new functions to support a wide range of applications. Although our discussion hasn't been an exhaustive account of all possible techniques that universal DBMS vendors employ to ensure their products perform well, we have focused on two major areas: support for new access methods or access method extensions, and support for influencing the data access strategy likely to be selected by the optimizer. Since universal DBMSs are still relatively new, it's likely that we'll see new performance tuning techniques introduced over time.

Some products have modified their indexing and optimization technologies to cope.

CHAPTER 8

Using Class Libraries

We've reviewed at length many features that make universal DBMSs extensible—user-defined types, user-defined functions, triggers, event alerters, new indexing technologies, and others. Such features provide the necessary building blocks for creating libraries of code to support new types of data and new forms of analysis involving that data. This chapter focuses on class libraries and their use in a universal DBMS environment.

Class libraries are building blocks for new applications.

What Are Class Libraries?

Object-oriented programming languages enable programmers to define new classes of objects, specifying both the characteristics (attributes) and operations (methods) associated with such objects. Such classes can be packaged as libraries and distributed for use by other programmers. Indeed, a number of independent software vendors offer class libraries for various programming languages. Some libraries target a specific industry, perhaps by providing functions useful to the finance, insurance, or health care industries. Others seek to be broadly applicable to multiple industries, perhaps by providing functions such as managing collections of data or interfacing to relational DBMSs.

They're similar to libraries found in object-oriented programming environments.

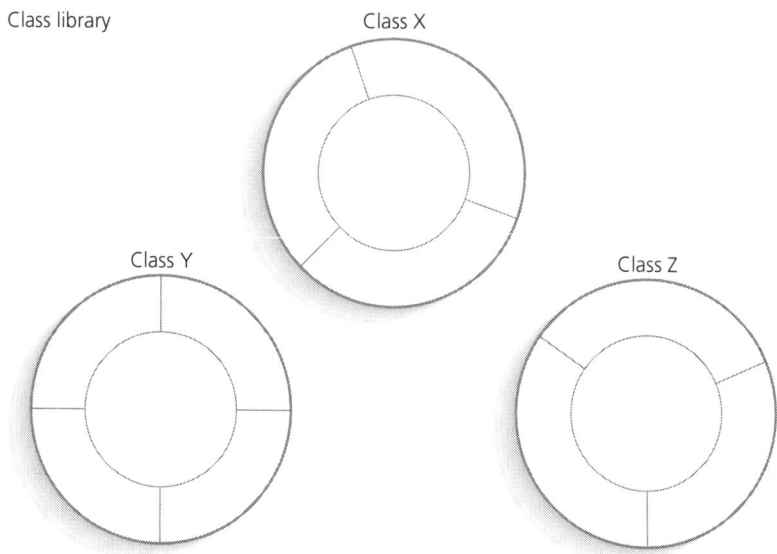

They consist of ready-made code that can cut application development time.

In any case, the appeal of class libraries is the same: they give firms the ability to purchase (or build) code that can readily be distributed and reused for multiple applications. Doing so can reduce overall application development time, ensure some degree of commonality across multiple projects, and enable firms to leverage the skills of specialists who built the class libraries.

In the DBMS world, these libraries are called Extenders, DataBlades, and so on.

Recognizing the value that class libraries can bring to object-oriented development projects, universal DBMS vendors have sought to offer a suite of similar libraries for their products. These libraries are marketed under various names, including DB2 Extenders (from IBM) and DataBlades (from Informix). Often priced separately from the base DBMS, these libraries provide ready-made support for specialized data types and functions.

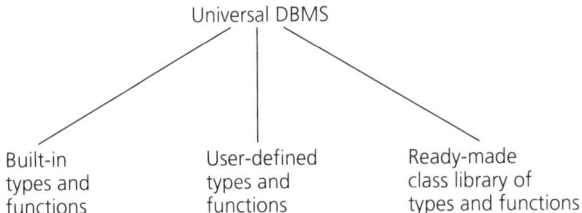

They consist of custom-built data types and functions that extend the capabilities of the DBMS product.

To build these class libraries, vendors make use of many universal DBMS features discussed earlier, including various forms of user-defined types, user-defined functions, and new indexing methods. Of course, the interfaces to these libraries are SQL-based. This enables firms to leverage existing SQL skills as well as easily incorporate new search criteria into their business queries. In some cases, class library builders undergo a certification process (by the universal DBMS vendor) to ensure their code behaves appropriately and meets predefined standards.

The interface to such libraries is still SQL-based.

We'll discuss a sampling of some of the class libraries provided for various universal DBMSs. But it's important to note that there's nothing to prevent firms from building their own class libraries using universal DBMS technology.

Firms can build their own libraries.

However, there can be practical limitations. Universal DBMSs are still relatively new, and no two products are identical. Building a class library—particularly one that introduces new indexing technology or other advanced features—requires solid programming skills and a good working knowledge of the target DBMS. This implies an investment of time and money in staff training. Some firms prefer to keep their IT staff focused on developing and maintaining applications specific to their businesses and to purchase "building block" software (such as class libraries) from vendors.

But buying commercial libraries may be more cost-effective.

Having said that, let's take a look at some of the class libraries available for commercial universal DBMSs.

Spatial Data Library

Spatial or geographic data is often supported via a class library.

Although "spatial data" sounds somewhat esoteric, its applicability to many commercial industries is rather wide. And that's perhaps easier to understand if we focus on the geographic (or geo-spatial) aspects of this kind of data.

Many aspects of business data have a geographic context.

Many forms of business data have some geographic element to them. Customer data includes addresses and phone numbers, both of which imply some location in physical space. Employees likewise have home addresses, commute via major roadways to a specific work address, and may regularly make use of the recreational, dining, and retail facilities within a certain distance of their homes or offices. Retailers and restaurateurs like to understand the demographics, transportation facilities, crime rates, and locations of competitors in the area immediately surrounding a new site that they may purchase or lease. Insurance companies like to understand the proximity of insured real estate to floodplains and earthquake faults, the crime rates of the surrounding region, and the values of comparable properties nearby.

To model spatial data, support for points, lines, and polygons is often needed.

To enable firms to factor geographic location into their business analysis, support for spatial data becomes important. And this support calls for new data types and functions to be introduced into the DBMS environment. A minimal set of data types may include the following:

- **Point data.** Points represent a specific location in space and are typically represented by x,y coordinates.

- **Line data.** Lines consist of two sets of points—one to represent the start of the line, and the other to represent the end of the line.
- **Polygon data.** Polygons represent regions in space. They can be represented in a variety of ways, including a set of points (pairs of which form the bounding lines of the region). For search purposes, the "minimum bounding rectangle" of a polygon is usually computed and tracked as a set of two points, representing the lower-left and upper-right corners of the rectangle.

The granularity of the reference map used for plotting this data affects what each data type might represent. For example, a map of the city of San Jose might represent the building at 555 Bailey Avenue as a single point, Bailey Avenue itself as a line, and the Santa Teresa district of San Jose as a polygon. However, on a map of the United States, San Jose itself might be represented as a single point, the state of California might be represented by a polygon, and Interstate Highway 80 might be represented by a line (or series of line segments).

These types can represent cities, homes, roadways, and more.

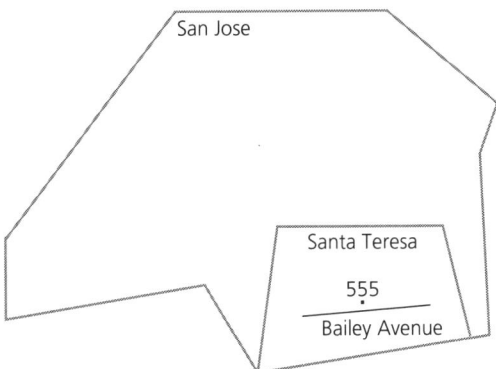

A map reference system is used for modeling purposes and to help assess relationships between geographic objects.

A number of functions are important to geographic analysis to test for distance, containment, and overlaps.

To complement these (and possibly other) data types included in a spatial library, a number of functions may be provided. These functions typically enable business users to understand the relationship between two or more spatial objects. Examples of spatial functions include the following:

- Determine the *distance* between two objects. For example, a retailer might wish to determine how far a new storefront is from the nearest freeway exit. This can involve computing the distance between two points.

- Determine if two objects *overlap*. For example, a construction company or an insurance firm might wish to determine if a planned housing development overlaps a known floodplain. This can involve evaluating the relationship between two different regions of geographic space.

- Determine if one object is contained *within* another object. For example, a home buyer might wish to determine if a given house is within a particular school district. This can involve evaluating the relationship between a point (the house) and a region (the school district) in space.

More complex types and functions may also be supported.

Of course, this isn't an exhaustive list. Other spatial functions are possible and supported in commercial class libraries. Indeed, additional data types are often supported as well, including complex polygons and line strings. A complex polygon might represent a polygon with a hole in it, such as a lake with an island inside or a US census district that excludes a certain number of blocks within an area. A line string might represent a line that crosses over itself, such as a patrol route.

But even with this limited discussion of spatial data, we can see that representing geographic information and enabling users to query on geographic relationships requires a reasonably rich set of types and functions. And, assuming that performance is important, spatial queries can require special indexing methods as well.

Many spatial libraries use new index techniques for performance.

As we discussed in Chapter 7, relational DBMSs typically support a B+-tree index structure. This structure is useful for many business queries and enables the DBMS to record values in the index that are based on one-dimensional data. But most spatial data is two-dimensional (at a minimum). Therefore, indexing spatial data requires using a structure that supports multidimensional values.

Various indexing techniques have been developed to speed searches involving spatial data, including R-trees (region trees), quad trees (quadrant trees), and grid file indexing. It's not uncommon for vendors of spatial class libraries to introduce a new indexing technology to the DBMS, along with new data types and functions.

Time Series Data Library

Information related to specific periods of time is another type of data common to many business environments. Brokerage firms need to understand the prices of stocks and commodities at various points in time to assess market trends and evaluate appropriate times for buying and selling interests in these items. Manufacturing firms need to understand peaks and valleys in production schedules, as well as relate projected schedules to purchases of equipment from suppliers. Retailers need to understand purchase patterns of their customers at different points in time, factoring in unusual events such as holidays and clearance sales.

Time series data is also important to many business applications.

In particular, data warehouse environments often require support for historical analysis.

Indeed, historical analysis is becoming increasingly popular in many industries, due in part to the growing interest in *data warehousing*. Data warehouses are a mechanism for storing information useful for decision support applications. Typically, this data is drawn from multiple data sources within the company and is appropriately restructured before being stored in the "warehouse," which is usually built on a relational DBMS. Part of the restructuring process involves resolving inconsistencies among the various online data sources from which warehouse information is drawn. Data transformation and cleansing operations are part of this process.

Consider a retailer who needs to understand customer buying patterns over time.

Data warehouses themselves typically contain historical data, as this information is relevant to many forms of business analysis. Again, think of a retailer trying to assess customer purchase patterns in order to determine what quantities of which goods should be stocked at various retail locations. It's important to understand not only what was purchased but when it was purchased and for how much. A similar case can be made in the finance industry, where understanding prices of stocks, bonds, and commodities over time can influence purchase decisions.

But not every industry has the same concept of time. Workweeks, for example, can vary considerably.

But perhaps what's not so obvious is that the concept of "time" varies across different application areas. In most countries, a workweek isn't the same as a calendar week. Indeed, defining working hours according to the "standard" US calendar of eight hours per day, Mondays through Fridays, is even too narrow. Holidays, which may vary somewhat in different regions, must be taken into consideration. Work hours and workdays can vary according to industry. And individual firms may shut down for certain periods of time, perhaps forcing paid or unpaid vacations to be taken for a brief time during the summer and/or winter. When we factor government and private educational institutions into the picture, the concept of a standard workday or work shift becomes even more elusive.

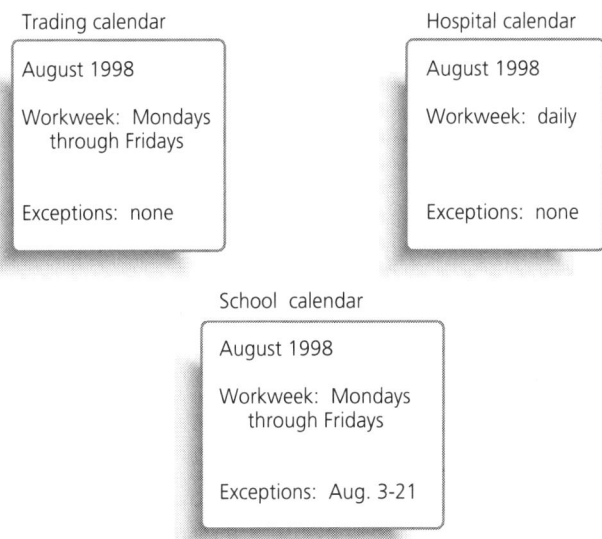

The ability to create and customize a calendar system is important for many queries.

Yet many forms of business analysis require time to be factored into queries in some way. A time series class library can help facilitate such queries by enabling companies to more easily represent historical data (as well as forecasts). This is accomplished by enabling firms to establish their own calendar systems and associated exceptions.

For example, a brokerage firm might establish a calendar for valid trading days, defined as Mondays through Fridays with the exception of certain holidays. Using this calendar, the firm could analyze fluctuations in stock prices over the 30-day trading period prior to January 1, 1999. Given US holidays, this period wouldn't be equivalent to all the days in December 1998.

Similarly, establishing a calendar system can help enforce integrity constraints. For example, if stock trading closes on Fridays, it makes no sense to allow users to insert new information about stock values for Saturdays and Sundays. By enabling firms to define their own

Calendar systems also provide additional data integrity.

valid calendaring systems for time series data, a class library can automate the enforcement of certain business rules.

Different calendar system implementations support different levels of frequency for time series data. Calendars may be defined on a subsecond basis through a yearly basis. In the stock-trading and retail examples we just discussed, a daily frequency would probably be most appropriate.

Most time series libraries include a variety of functions.

Of course, class libraries that support time series data also provide functions that facilitate temporal analysis of that data. Again, specific functions supported vary from offering to offering. But examples include computing the maximum and minimum values for an element within a specified time range, computing the moving average for an element within a given time range, extracting an element of a time series based on a specific date, and determining if one element is always greater than another element within a specific time series. Such functions can be useful for determining the high and low values of a stock within a period of time, the moving average of a stock within a period of time, the value of a stock at a specific point in time, and an analysis of whether or not stock A always closed at a higher value than stock B during a period of time.

Text Data Library

Full text is another common form of business data.

Full-text documents are a common form of business data traditionally supported by specialized DBMS products, including text retrieval systems and document management systems. It's not uncommon for firms to try to integrate full-text data with other forms of business data for decision support applications.

For example, personnel organizations may wish to store resumes and reference letters along with information about job applicants' career interests, desired salary range, and date of application. For current employees, personnel staff might like to record serial numbers, names, number of dependents, current assignments, salaries, and recent performance appraisal reports. Process manuals, marketing collateral, internal memos, trip reports, and operations reports are additional examples of full-text documents that contain important business data.

Resumes, appraisals, marketing collateral, and memos are all examples.

Employee information

Serial # : 764
Name: David Mario
Dependents: 5
Assignment: Manager
Salary: 65,000
Resume:
xxx xx
xxxxx
xxx xx

Appraisal:
xxx x
xxxx
x xxx

Often, text needs to be combined with more traditional forms of business data.

Not surprisingly, text data was among the first types of data supported for universal DBMSs via class libraries. A text class library can enable firms to search on keywords, word synonyms, and word derivatives (or word stems) within an electronic document. Incorporating Boolean logic into a search is also typically supported; an example might include searching resumes for mention of "Java" and "UNIX."

But text data requires its own search functions and techniques.

Synonyms, fuzzy matches, and proximity may need to be considered.

Depending on the offering in question, more sophisticated text search capabilities may be supported as well. The software may support fuzzy matching, be capable of ranking matching documents in terms of their relevance to the search criteria, and filter results based on the proximity of two terms to one another.

Text libraries typically do this. Some support multiple languages.

English is the most common natural language supported by text class libraries, although some support a number of other languages as well (including languages that employ double-byte character sets). To help firms integrate existing documents into a universal DBMS environment, some text libraries also support import facilities for common document formats, such as ASCII text, Microsoft Word, Adobe Acrobat, and others.

Most introduce new indexing techniques to speed performance.

To ensure reasonable performance of queries involving full-text data, class library vendors often include custom indexing technology with their products. Because document management systems and text retrieval systems have been marketed commercially for years, significant research investment has been made in techniques to speed searches of text data. Again, traditional B+-tree indexes aren't particularly useful for this form of data, so various other indexing strategies are employed by vendors of text class libraries to meet performance goals.

Image Data Library

The World Wide Web has helped increase the use of image data at many firms.

Electronic images are another form of data supported via class libraries. In recent years, the ability to manage, search, and integrate image data with other forms of business data has become of greater importance in a number of industries. Part of this is due to the advent of the World Wide Web, in which Web pages for marketing and electronic commerce applications increasingly feature graphics for added visual appeal.

Often, image data is closely associated with other forms of traditional business data. For example, mail order firms as well as retailers with electronic storefronts (on Web pages) must associate images of their products with prices, order numbers, descriptions, and ordering information. Enabling employees or potential customers to search on both image content and traditional attributes (such as pricing) can be important to satisfy market demands.

For example, a Web-based catalog can require image data to be supplemented by more traditional data types.

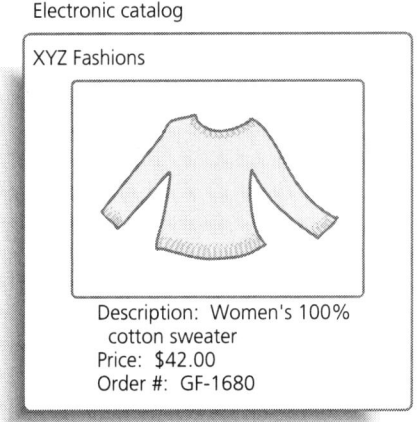

Similarly, insurance firms may benefit from maintaining electronic images of insured properties along with policy information. Images of damaged property may be appropriate to record when claims are filed. Finally, any organization maintaining a digital library of photos or artwork—such as government agencies, museums, and art galleries—could potentially benefit from an image class library.

Images of various formats may be imported into a universal DBMS. Sometimes attribute data is extracted automatically.

Image libraries are typically designed to support a variety of file formats, such as GIF, JPEG, BMP, and TIFF. Thus, external image data can be imported into a DBMS environment, where it can be managed, shared, and searched along with other forms of business data. Some libraries provide for automatic extraction of certain image attributes when images are added to the database. This extraction can be useful, as it captures criteria that users may wish to incorporate into searches. Examples include the height and width of the image or the format of the image.

Searching by image content can be a valuable function of a class library.

Of course, it's likely that a broader range of search criteria is required for image data. Many class libraries support content-based searches, in which users can search for images based on color, pattern, and other criteria. This might be useful for searching electronic catalogs for images that are like other images—perhaps to order table linens to match a drapery pattern. As with text libraries, image libraries often support relevancy ranking, returning a "hit list" of images ranked in order of how closely they match the query criteria.

Additional functions may be provided as well.

In addition to providing functions that support content-based searches, image libraries also provide functions to alter or work with images in other ways. Examples include cropping, rotating, and flipping images. To conserve disk space, some offerings also can compress data for storage. The degree of potential data loss and the expense of decompressing data for retrieval are administrative considerations when deciding whether or not image data should be compressed for storage.

Video Data Library

Video data is one of the newer forms to be supported commercially.

Most discussions of image class libraries ultimately lead to questions about video class libraries. A number of offerings enable video data to be integrated in a universal DBMS environment, although the business requirement for such support has been limited to date. While it's true that video clips are more frequently being integrated into Web pages and that video data is of considerable importance to the entertainment industry, a broad need for video data is less clear.

However, firms that seek to integrate such data with other forms of business data will find class libraries on the market to support this activity. Since video data is commonly stored outside a DBMS, class libraries usually provide interfaces to popular file formats, which may include MPEG-1, AVI, and Quicktime. As with image class libraries, some video class libraries can automatically extract attribute data when videos are imported into DBMS-managed tables. Again, this is useful when these attributes are often used for search criteria. Examples of attributes that may be extracted from video files include the length of the video, the frame rate, the number of frames, and the compression method used.

Again, interfaces to popular file formats are often provided.

Searches are often done on attributes associated with video data.

Because of the size associated with video data, some class libraries enable video data to remain in separate file servers but still be managed and searched by a universal DBMS. In such cases, support for good administrative facilities is important and should be built into the class library itself.

Other Class Libraries

A number of other class libraries are already available for various universal DBMSs. While it's beyond the scope of this book to list and explain them all, it's worthwhile to at least mention a few:

Libraries are also available for other types of data.

- **Web class library.** Such a library may allow Web applications and/or Web pages to be stored and managed by the universal DBMS. Support for management of multiple data types may be included. Examples here include Java applets, HTML or SGML files, and SQL queries.

- **Audio class library.** Such a library enables firms to store audio data in their DBMS. Import facilities to popular audio file formats may be provided. Various forms of analysis and searching may be supported, including content-based searches and classification according to pitch, tone, and other audio qualities.

Some even focus more on function than specific data types.

- **Data cleansing library.** Such a library is probably most useful to firms attempting to construct data warehouses and data marts. Bringing together data from various sources often requires "scrubbing" the data to resolve inconsistencies, such as different spellings of what may be one customer's name or different mailing addresses for the same employee. Routines to help firms through this process are part of a data cleansing library.

Class Libraries and Industry Standards

However, commercial offerings aren't standardized.

As you may have guessed, class libraries for universal DBMSs vary considerably from vendor to vendor. The features of one vendor's spatial library can differ considerably from another's. Moreover, the interface surfaced to programmers and users—via the user-defined functions supported in the class library—also differ.

The SQL committee is working on defining standards for managing various forms of nontraditional data, such as full-text, spatial, and still image data. After these standards are defined, it's possible that class library vendors will strive to be compliant. This would bring a greater level of consistency across the industry to libraries of a given type.

Summary

Although universal DBMSs are still relatively new offerings, a number of class libraries have already emerged for these products. Class libraries are prepackaged code that include new data types and new functions to help firms integrate various forms of business data in a single environment. Although available class libraries vary depending on the DBMS in question, support for spatial data, time series data, image data, and full-text data is relatively common. Other libraries may feature support for audio data, video data, and Web data. Some even focus on providing a collection of useful functions that is largely independent of data types, such as the data cleansing library discussed earlier.

Although firms can certainly build their own libraries using mechanisms such as user-defined types and user-defined functions, it's often more cost-effective to purchase a ready-made class library. Doing so eliminates much of the in-house development effort that would have to take place—an effort that could involve substantial time and skill if performance, integrity, and storage management issues are to be taken into consideration. However, it's wise to closely evaluate a class library before purchase, as two libraries that support spatial data or text data can vary significantly.

But class libraries still offer firms a quick start when it comes to working with unusual data types.

CHAPTER 9

Distributed Data, Universally Managed

W e've seen how universal DBMSs can provide a central facility for storing, managing, and analyzing many forms of data. But what happens if your data isn't all in one place? Can universal DBMS technology cope with data in external file systems or data that is physically distributed across multiple platforms?

Let's consider how universal DBMS technology can be applied to data that isn't all in one place.

This chapter explores these questions, focusing on two emerging technologies available in some universal DBMSs to cope with management of distributed data. These technologies are file links and multidatabase servers. As of this writing, standardization efforts for file links are still in the proposal stage, and much of the technology for multidatabase servers falls outside the scope of standards efforts. So our discussions will draw on commercial implementations.

File Links for Managing External Data

Class libraries and underlying universal DBMS features (such as user-defined types and functions) enable firms to store many kinds of data directly in DBMS-managed tables. In some cases, import facilities are even provided to read data stored in popular formats and convert this data into a format acceptable to the DBMS.

One option involves linking external files to DBMS-managed tables.

Some products also support the concept of a *file link,* which allows data to remain outside the DBMS in native file formats but still be managed by the DBMS in various ways. The idea here is to extend the value of universal DBMS technology outside its immediate domain, so that integrity, security, and recovery mechanisms can be applied both to DBMS-managed data and external files. File links are designed to work independent of file type, so they can potentially link DBMS tables to intranet Web pages, engineering drawings, interoffice memos, service manuals, training videos, and other files.

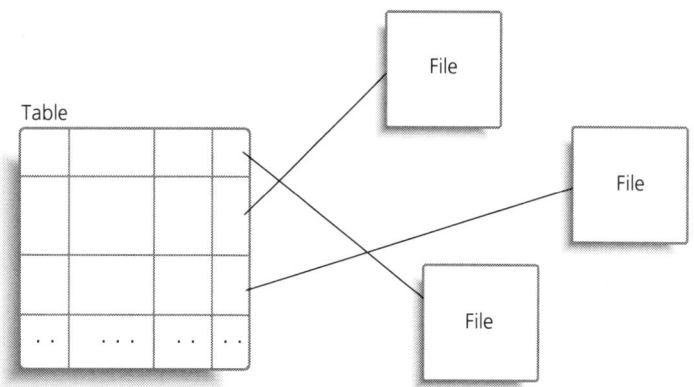

A column is defined in the table to contain a "file link."

But if a universal DBMS can manage many types of data, why would anyone want some data to remain in separate files?

Business Value

This approach can be useful if importing file data isn't practical.

Allowing data to remain in external files while bringing these files under the universal DBMS "umbrella" offers firms additional administrative flexibility and control. In most companies, a large amount of data still exists in file systems, and a large number of applications are dependent on data in these files. Yet often, data in these files may be related to (or even dependent upon) DBMS-managed data.

Migrating the data from files to the DBMS can be labor-intensive and require costly rewrites of applications designed to interface to these files. Furthermore, if the DBMS is remote from the application, migrating the data further away could cause performance to degrade. Copying the data into the DBMS introduces concerns about efficient use of IT resources and data synchronization issues. Finally, some firms have purchased specialized servers to ensure efficient delivery of data stored in files; video servers, which must stream data to clients within a given time, are one example of this. Again, migrating the data out of files could be an unacceptable compromise.

It allows existing applications to access the files as usual.

However, equally unacceptable may be trying to write custom software to ensure that the relationship between data resident in a DBMS and data resident in a file is maintained. Presumably, if a table contains information about suppliers of parts and these parts are included in an external computer-aided design file, we might not want that file to be deleted without making some appropriate change to the table. Similarly, we might want to ensure that backup and recovery processes are coordinated between the DBMS and the appropriate files.

But it provides additional administrative control and greater integrity.

The notion behind file links is to provide software to manage such situations automatically. As such, file links provide additional administrative facilities that span beyond the DBMS itself.

Finally, by bringing external files under the wing of a universal DBMS, firms can provide their SQL programmers and users with access to data that they might not have otherwise known existed. Although the data may be physically stored separately, DBMS users can have a greater chance of integrating this data into their applications should they need to do so.

Typical Capabilities

File links are rather new.

Because file link technology is relatively new, it's difficult to define "typical" capabilities associated with this function. However, we can discuss features available commercially, such as the DataLinks technology integrated in IBM's DB2 Universal Database.

The link itself usually employs a URL format common in Web environments.

As mentioned previously, file links enable a universal DBMS to extend its management services to external files. This is accomplished by enabling users to create tables with one or more columns that contain file links. The file link specifies the full path and location of the external file, often using the Uniform Resource Locator (URL) convention common in Web-based environments. (For example, a file link may have a format of *http://servername/pathname/filename.*)

Here's how we might create a table with a file link.

The following statement shows how a PRODUCT table can be created to track products marketed by a firm. This table might contain columns for each product's order number, description, and image. In this case, image data is stored externally as a file, so the column's data type is a DATALINK that uses a URL-based format to store information about the external file's location. DATALINK is a new data type introduced into DB2 Universal Database to manage external files.

```
CREATE TABLE PRODUCT
(ORDER_NO      INTEGER,
 DESCRIPTION   VARCHAR(50),
 IMAGE         DATALINK (60) LINKTYPE URL
 . . .
)
```

PRODUCT

ORDER_NO	DESCRIPTION	IMAGE
654	Wool Blazer	<URL> → External file
...	...	...

But just being able to store information about a file's location in a table isn't that exciting. File links also enable administrators to specify integrity, security, and recovery constraints for the files. Specific capabilities can affect the following:

- **Referential integrity constraints.** For example, a file link can ensure that external files aren't deleted or renamed while they're referenced by the DBMS. Among other things, this prevents "broken pointers"—or inaccurate/outdated file references—from being stored in the DBMS.

- **Read/write permissions.** Read permissions for the file can be managed by the DBMS (through standard SQL mechanisms) or left with the file system. Write permissions can be left with the file system or "blocked" so that users cannot update a referenced file in place. Blocked files have the advantage of allowing for backup and recovery operations that are coordinated by the DBMS. To update a blocked file, users can create a new file (or new version of the same file), cause the old file to be "unlinked" from the table, and have the new version linked into the table (by having its URL stored in the row).

- **Backup and recovery.** The DBMS can be made responsible for coordinating backup and recovery operations for user data stored in tables as well as referenced data stored in external files.

- **Transaction consistency.** Transactions in a DBMS environment are logical units of work. Either all activities within a transaction

Links can be more than just a tracking mechanism.

They enable a universal DBMS to apply integrity, security, and recovery controls over external data.

must be applied to the database, or none must be applied. File links extend the notion of transaction consistency to external files, ensuring that COMMIT and ROLLBACK operations apply to appropriate external files as well as to data stored in tables.

With these capabilities in mind, the following statement is a more complete example of how the PRODUCT table mentioned previously can be created with a column that contains a file link.

```
CREATE TABLE PRODUCT
(ORDER_NO       INTEGER,
DESCRIPTION    VARCHAR(50), +
IMAGE          DATALINK (60) LINKTYPE URL
FILE LINK CONTROL
   INTEGRITY ALL
   READ PERMISSION DB
   WRITE PERMISSION BLOCKED
   RECOVERY YES
   ON UNLINK RESTORE
)
```

Here's a more detailed look at some of these administrative options.

To give you some idea of the capabilities associated with file links, let's examine each file link control statement more closely. The INTEGRITY ALL line specifies that the DBMS is to manage the integrity constraints associated with the file, which include not allowing the file to be deleted if a table references it. Next, we see that the DBMS will manage security privileges for read operations—not the file system. For write operations, direct updates to the file in place are blocked. Instead, a new file or a copy of the existing file can be made and changed. Then, an SQL UPDATE operation can be performed referencing the new or changed file.

The final two lines specify that recovery operations are to be managed by the DBMS and that when a file is unlinked from a table (perhaps because a row was deleted), control over the file is to be restored to the native file system. Alternatively, an administrator could have specified that the file should be automatically deleted.

Now that we've seen how tables with links to external files can be created, let's consider how programmers and users can interact with them. The standard SQL operations for manipulating data still apply: INSERT, UPDATE, DELETE, and SELECT. In other words, users can access and change the contents of the file link column (the URL) through standard database operations. Therefore, a statement such as this would return information about the image file associated with product number 145.

Users still write SQL to work with tables that contain file links.

```
SELECT IMAGE
FROM PRODUCT
WHERE ORDER_NO = 145
```

Accessing and manipulating the file itself—in this case the image for product 145—is accomplished by standard file system calls. It's *not* done through SQL. This is an area in which file links differ from class libraries that create new types and functions for images in a universal DBMS environment. However, some firms may be able to code user-defined functions for file link data if SQL access is desired.

But working with the external files themselves involves using native file interfaces.

By contrast, the class library approach calls for the images themselves to be stored in a user database—not as an external file (and possibly a remote file at that). Furthermore, images stored in the database are accessed and manipulated through SQL, not the file system's API. As we've already discussed in Chapter 8, image class libraries typically introduce a number of new user-defined functions to enable firms to work with images stored in tables.

With file links, the images (or other data) reside in external files and are manipulated by the standard interfaces provided for the file system in question. The DBMS merely stores a link to that file—

often in URL format—and enables users to query and manipulate that link as they would any other DBMS-managed data.

Sample Architecture

File links require additional software to reside on systems that contain external files.

At this point, you may be wondering just how the file link mechanism works. After all, if a universal DBMS is managing recovery, integrity, and security for files, doesn't some software need to be installed on the target system to coordinate activities with the DBMS?

The answer is yes. Part of this architecture calls for a software layer to reside on the same system as the external file so that it can trap appropriate user and DBMS activities in order to act as needed. As we saw earlier, administrators have the option of specifying that read permissions for the external file are to be controlled by the DBMS. To achieve this, a software layer traps user attempts to open the file so that authorization can be checked by the DBMS.

Of course, the software layer does more than just that. If recovery is to be coordinated with the DBMS, the file link software layer must also be responsible for backing up and recovering external files when appropriate. When an external file is "linked" to a database table (perhaps as a result of an INSERT operation), the file is backed up asynchronously to the transaction. When a database backup operation is performed, the DBMS ensures that all necessary file backups have been completed and records information about this to facilitate recovery. In this way, the database and corresponding files can be restored to the level of a particular backup. Roll forward processing can also be performed on the database and external files in a coordinated manner.

The following figure depicts the architecture associated with one commercial offering (from IBM) that supports file links. Applications use SQL to communicate with the universal DBMS, accessing business data stored in tables. This includes the URLs of external files managed by the DBMS. Standard file system commands are used to work with the external files, unless firms have created user-defined functions for this purpose. A software layer (called DataLinker) is responsible for communicating with the DBMS as well as intercepting certain user activities.

This software communicates with the DBMS and intercepts certain user actions as appropriate.

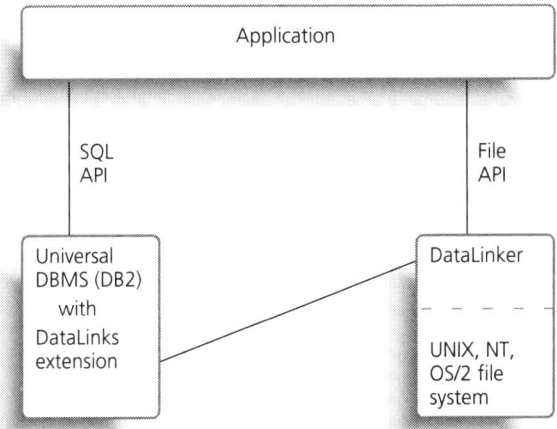

Here's the architecture used by one commercial product to support file links.

Multidatabase Servers

While file links enable firms to associate DBMS-managed tables with external files, multidatabase servers provide firms with a single-site image of data that is stored in various formats, often across various systems. Products in this area—available from IBM, Sybase, and others—are variously called hub servers, federated database management systems, next-generation gateways, and data access middleware.

Working with distributed data can also be accomplished by building a "virtual database."

But regardless of what they're called, such products have begun enabling object/relational technology to be globally applied to a variety of back-end data sources. They create a *virtual database* comprised of many disparate data sources.

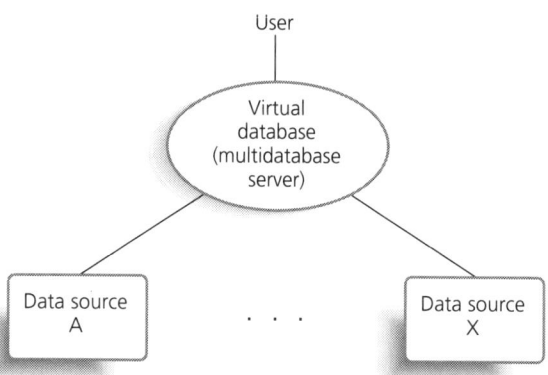

Users perceive data stored in different formats on different systems as if they were part of a single database.

Multidatabase servers are products that support this.

Multidatabase servers offer a consistent application programming interface (API) to select flat files as well as relational, object/relational, and prerelational DBMSs. The interface may support both embedded SQL as well as a call-level interface that conforms to Microsoft's Open Database Connectivity (ODBC) specification. Both read and write access may be supported, including the ability to join data from multiple sources in a single SQL statement or update data in multiple sources with integrity. However, some data access restrictions typically apply.

Transparent access is a key goal.

But what's interesting about virtual databases is that they enable users and programmers to transparently access disparate data that is physically dispersed throughout a network. Often, the virtual database server can compensate for differences among the various data sources and simulate function not available natively on the back end. Such functions can include support for user-defined types, user-defined functions, and other object/relational technologies associated with universal DBMSs.

In some ways, then, vendors are already applying universal DBMS technology beyond a single DBMS environment. This very idea introduces a new dimension to the word "universal." But before we delve into what multidatabase servers are all about, let's consider the value they might bring to IT environments.

Some products in this area are built on universal DBMS technology.

Business Value

Multidatabase servers can help simplify a complex IT environment for programmers and end users, as well as improve access to remote data. Part of this simplicity stems from eliminating the need for users to learn multiple interfaces to multiple data sources or even be aware that needed data is stored on multiple systems. Enabling users to work at a higher level of abstraction allows them to concentrate on the business problem at hand rather than struggle to cope with environment-specific issues, including multiple APIs, multiple networking protocols, data type translation services, and code page conversions (for national language support).

Simplified access to disparate data sources is one benefit.

Some firms also view multidatabase servers as a means to help them protect application investments in an ever-changing IT environment. Traditionally, application programmers have incorporated product-specific calls in their applications to access data. These calls can include DL/1 statements for accessing IMS data, Transact-SQL statements for accessing Sybase SQL Server data, PL/SQL statements for accessing Oracle data, or other vendor-specific SQL dialects for accessing other relational DBMS data.

Insulating applications from changing IT environments is another.

Of course, doing so makes the application dependent on the data source. If something prompts a firm to consider migrating to a new data source, these applications will have to be rewritten. And application rewrites are an expensive proposition that companies would rather avoid.

Multidatabase servers can help decrease a firm's dependency on a specific data source. By writing to a single interface, programmers become insulated from vendor-specific SQL dialects and other native interfaces. Thus, if data is migrated from one source to another, applications are less likely to require change. Of course, a common concern with this approach is that firms become dependent on the multidatabase server. Fortunately, most support de facto or de jure SQL standards, so the risk of getting "locked in" by a multidatabase server vendor is minimized.

Applying new functions to existing data sources is also beneficial.

Support for *functional compensation* offers firms the potential of applying advanced technologies to existing data sources that may not evolve to include such enhancements. As we'll discuss, some multidatabase server products now enable users to apply object/relational features to file systems, prerelational DBMSs, and relational DBMSs that do not support such extensions natively. Doing so enables firms to leverage their existing IT investments in new ways.

This technology can also facilitate decision support and data warehousing environments.

Finally, companies use multidatabase servers for reasons not directly related to universal DBMS technology. These reasons include the following:

- ■ **Data propagation and replication services.** These services enable users to maintain copies of data in multiple sources. Improved performance and data availability for local applications are reasons that motivate firms to use replication facilities.

- ■ **Data transformation for data warehousing.** Multidatabase servers can provide a transient storage mechanism for operational data pulled from multiple sources. After integrating, transforming, and cleansing the data as needed, users can then copy this data to a data mart or data warehouse. Some multidatabase servers support local storage of data, enabling them to serve as a warehouse "engine" for decision support applications.

- **A virtual warehouse.** Here, the multidatabase server simulates a global warehouse where none exists. This can be useful if numerous data marts are in place and some users need access to data stored in multiple marts.

- **Elimination of individual database gateways.** Gateway technology dates back to the 1980s and involves point-to-point access, usually between two DBMSs. Some gateways, such as those supporting mainframe access, can be quite costly. Others suffer from functional limitations and data access restrictions. Multidatabase servers offer an alternative to such products.

In some cases, it can even help reduce costs.

Typical Capabilities

While a number of multidatabase servers are available commercially, a relatively small percentage of these enable universal DBMS technology to be applied to disparate back-end data sources. This makes it difficult to discuss "typical" capabilities of products in this area. However, we'll try to make some generalizations. And when necessary, we'll draw on examples from one commercial offering (IBM's DB2 DataJoiner) that has made global application of object/relational extensions an area of emphasis.

Access to file systems and various types of DBMSs is usually supported.

Basic features of multidatabase servers often include the following:

- **Transparent access to a variety of data sources,** including file systems, relational DBMSs, and nonrelational DBMSs. Some implementations enable data to be read from multiple sources in a single query (such as a join or union). Less common, but occasionally supported, is the ability to update data in multiple sources in a single transaction with automatic two-phase commit support to ensure integrity.

SQL is the common interface.

- **Support for ODBC and/or ANSI/ISO embedded SQL interfaces.** These are widely accepted application programming interfaces for accessing relational data. Multidatabase servers allow these interfaces to be applied to relational and nonrelational data sources.

- **Support for a "pass through" mechanism.** This enables programmers to use the native interface of a particular data source. This feature is helpful if a vendor-specific capability needs to be exploited, but its use compromises transparent access.

- **Client/server or multitier architecture.** Multidatabase servers must cope with networked environments. Typically, they're installed in multitier configurations, with desktop clients connecting to a multidatabase server via a LAN, and the multidatabase server connecting to multiple local and remote data sources on the clients' behalf.

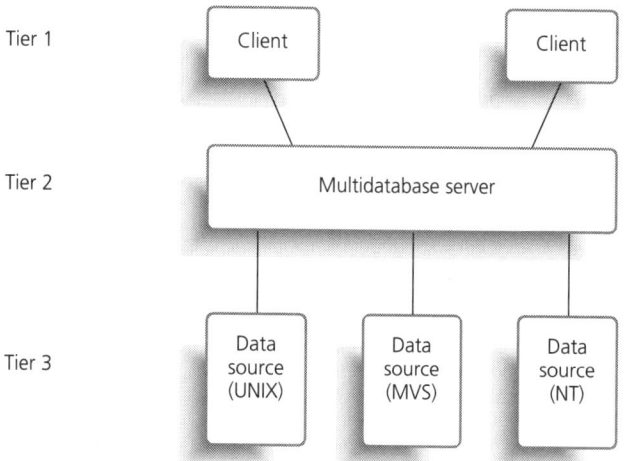

The environment is inherently networked.

Other advanced functions are sometimes supported as well. Again, these can vary considerably from product to product. But briefly, they may include the following:

- **Global optimization.** Resolving requests that span multiple data sources implies a need for smart data access strategies. Many multidatabase servers include an optimizer that evaluates different alternatives for resolving a query and selects a low-cost option to ensure reasonable performance.

- **Global catalog.** Selecting an efficient data access strategy requires the ability to assess costs of various alternatives. In relational and universal DBMSs, statistical data is collected and stored in a series of catalog tables. The optimizer consults this data to determine likely costs of different access strategies. Some multidatabase servers maintain an extended catalog that contains statistical data from back-end data sources as well as information about network connections and CPU speeds.

- **Local storage.** Some multidatabase servers embed a full-function DBMS. Therefore, they're able to store data locally in tables, as well as access data in back-end sources.

- **Data replication services.** In addition to supporting access to "live" data stored in various systems, some multidatabase servers include integrated replication or copy management services. These services allow data to be copied among the various back-end sources in an automated fashion.

- **Web interfaces.** A number of multidatabase servers can support query and report writing in Web-based environments.

- **Functional compensation.** This involves the ability to simulate certain functions not natively supported by back-end data sources. Global support of object/relational technology—a feature provided by some multidatabase servers—is usually accomplished through functional compensation.

Advanced features focus on performance, local storage of data, copy management services, and functional compensation.

Some products can simulate universal DBMS functions on top of data sources that don't support them natively.

Let's take a closer look at this broad area of functional compensation, as it represents a way of extending universal DBMS technology beyond a local database environment and into a global one. Of course, other forms of functional compensation are also possible, but that's not the subject of this book.

As we've already discussed, some multidatabase servers are built on a full-function DBMS engine. In effect, these products represent an extension of existing database technology—an extension that focuses on supporting heterogeneous data access. When the underlying base is a universal or object/relational DBMS, the multidatabase server may be extended to support user-defined types, user-defined functions, stored procedures, and other features across multiple data sources. Indeed, this is the approach adopted by DataJoiner.

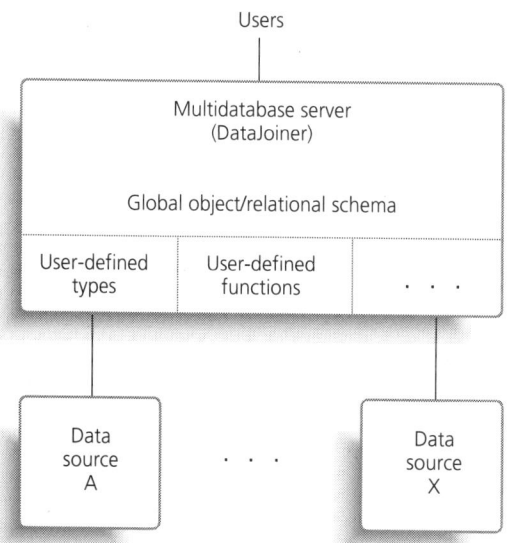

Recall the discussion of user-defined types in Chapters 3 and 4. There, we saw how universal DBMSs can enable users to create new types of data, including both simple and complex types. Strong typing enforces additional integrity constraints, preventing invalid comparisons and other operations.

Some multidatabase servers enable users to create new data types and map these types to a back-end data source. If data in the back-end source is accessed only through the multidatabase server, the integrity features associated with strong typing are automatically enforced. This prevents nonsensical operations from occurring, even if the underlying data source has no native understanding of the valid behaviors associated with the data type.

The usefulness of such a feature is potentially greater if applied to multiple data sources. Consider a situation in which two different DBMSs have tables containing financial information, including account balances. Perhaps the BALANCE columns were even both defined with the same data type. However, one table contains values in Canadian dollars, while the other contains values in US dollars.

Obviously, a direct comparison would be misleading. But without user-defined types and strong typing, such a comparison would be considered valid by the system. A multidatabase server that supports heterogeneous application of universal DBMS technology can be of help here. An administrator could define separate data types for CANADIAN_DOLLARs and US_DOLLARs to the multidatabase server and map these to the appropriate remote tables. Any attempts to query these tables through the multidatabase server and compare values of these columns would be recognized as invalid.

New types (and associated operational restrictions) can be defined for multiple data sources.

This can prevent certain integrity violations from occurring.

User-defined functions and other features may be supported as well.

Similarly, some multidatabase servers enable users to create their own functions and apply these functions to relational and nonrelational back-end data sources. Doing so extends the range of possible operations that can be performed on these data sources. It also can contribute to enforcing consistent behavior and a consistent, global interface to data. Finally, large objects and stored procedures are other features that may be supported by a multidatabase server.

Sample Architecture

At this point, you may be wondering just how multidatabase servers are able to accomplish these ambitious goals. A closer examination of the components of a multidatabase server will shed some light on this. Again, implementations do vary from product to product. We'll try to keep this discussion as broadly applicable as possible. But when that's not possible, we'll lean toward discussing commercial offerings that support object/relational technology, such as DataJoiner.

Multidatabase servers may provide an API, a DBMS engine, and a number of data source interfaces.

We've already touched on some of the components found in multidatabase servers, such as a global optimizer and global catalog. Let's step back and look at multidatabase servers from a user's perspective. When we do, we can identify three major elements of interest:

1. The application programming interface (API)
2. The multidatabase server engine
3. Interfaces to various back-end data sources

Multidatabase Servers

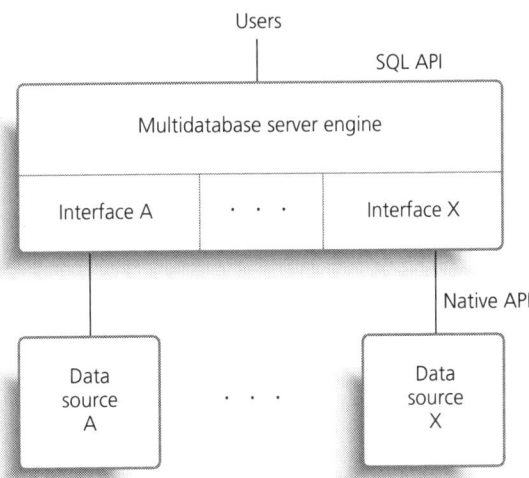

Here's a sample architecture. Users write to one **SQL-based API** and connect to the multidatabase server. Data source interfaces work with the back ends.

Application programming interface. As we've mentioned, the API is SQL-based. Both ODBC and embedded SQL approaches are often supported. And while most vendors strive to comply with industry standards, object/relational extensions are still relatively new. Therefore, some vendor-specific SQL extensions may be featured to support advanced functions. In some implementations, considerable support is provided for transparent read access. A few also provide for multisite updates in a single transaction, although back-end data sources that can participate in such scenarios may be limited.

Both ODBC and embedded SQL interfaces may be supported.

Multidatabase server engine. The engine component is arguably the most critical, as its technology can impact performance, integrity, and other issues. Some multidatabase server engines are extended versions of relational or universal DBMSs. As such, they support both real databases (with locally stored tables) as well as virtual databases (in which data is physically distributed across a network and often stored in multiple formats).

The DBMS engine is the heart of this technology.

Because performance is often critical, the engine must be able to determine an efficient data access strategy.

Optimization and performance tuning mechanisms fall within the domain of the multidatabase server engine. Some vendors have invested heavily in optimization technology to ensure that user requests for distributed data are handled in an efficient manner, minimizing network traffic, I/O, sorts, and other expensive operations. We've already mentioned that consulting statistics about global data can help the optimizer make a well-informed decision about how to process a user's query. Additional techniques supported in some commercial offerings include query rewrite processing and push-down analysis. We'll discuss each very briefly here.

Various optimization techniques make this possible.

Some relational and universal optimizers can automatically transform poorly written queries into equivalent forms that are more efficient to process. This is an important performance consideration, as not all programmers are SQL experts. Furthermore, some application development and query tools enable users to graphically construct database requests, generating SQL statements automatically. Unfortunately, not all tools generate the most efficient forms of SQL for all data sources. Built-in support for query rewrite processing can help in both cases.

Here's an example of one technique involving query rewrites.

To illustrate how this works, consider an EMPLOYEE table with columns for employee ID, name, job title, and salary. Assume that a unique index has been created on the ID column to ensure that no duplicate rows appear in this table.

```
EMPLOYEE TABLE:
   ID, NAME, JOBTITLE, SALARY

EMP_INX INDEX:
   UNIQUE INDEX ON "ID" COLUMN OF EMPLOYEE TABLE
```

Consider what might occur if the following SQL statement were issued. This statement retrieves the ID and name of each employee whose annual salary is greater than $75,000.

```
SELECT DISTINCT ID, NAME
FROM EMPLOYEE
WHERE SALARY > 75000
```

The DISTINCT clause is part of standard SQL. It specifies that duplicate rows in the answer set are to be eliminated. DBMSs typically achieve this by retrieving all qualifying rows and then sorting them so that duplicates can be removed. However, the DISTINCT clause—and a corresponding sort—is superfluous here, since the unique index on the ID column guarantees that no duplicate ID values exist. An optimizer that supports query rewrite processing can detect this situation and rewrite the query as follows to eliminate the DISTINCT and avoid a sort.

```
SELECT ID, NAME
FROM EMPLOYEE
WHERE SALARY > 75000
```

Many more sophisticated forms of query rewrite processing are possible; some have already been implemented commercially. But it's the concept here that's important. Multidatabase servers sometimes incorporate this technology to ensure reasonable performance in a distributed environment. Indeed, some relational DBMSs also feature this capability, but it's applied to locally managed data rather than distributed data managed by different data sources.

Push-down analysis involves examining the operations required to process a user's query with the objective of ensuring that work involving a given data source is processed as close to the data as possible. In other words, data filtering operations are "pushed down" to a back-end source to avoid unnecessary network traffic and improve performance.

Applying data filters close to the data source also helps.

Performance tuning mechanisms can vary from product to product. But it's not unusual for a multidatabase server to enable users to view the access strategy selected by the global optimizer to satisfy a request. In some cases, users may also be able to view the access strategies employed by the back-end data sources to process their portions of the work. Reviewing the access strategy can help programmers fine-tune their queries as well as give administrators insights into database design changes that may help improve performance, such as the addition of a new index.

> **Data source interfaces handle translation work automatically.**

Data source interfaces. The final elements of this architecture of importance to users are the interfaces to back-end data sources. A different interface (or "driver") is typically written for each data source. This component is responsible for translating SQL into the native interface of the back-end data source. Translating data types and return codes between the data source and multidatabase server engine is also the responsibility of the interface component.

> **It's important to understand what back-end interfaces are supported.**

Data source interfaces affect the number and types of back-end sources supported by a multidatabase server. If an interface to a necessary data source isn't available for your multidatabase server, you may not be able to make that data accessible to your users in this environment. Some products include tool kits to enable users to build their own custom interfaces to various data sources. However, the process of doing so often requires considerable skill. It's best to settle on a product that offers ready-made support to the data sources you need.

Summary

This chapter has examined two ways in which the "universal" aspect of a universal DBMS can take on new meaning, largely because the range of managed data can extend beyond a single, local system. File links, for example, enable a DBMS to manage local tables that reference external files. Furthermore, some management functions can be applied to these files, such as coordinated backup and recovery, referential integrity enforcement, and security.

Multidatabase servers can provide a *virtual* universal DBMS environment. They offer users a single-site image of data that is physically dispersed throughout an organization, often stored in different data formats. Furthermore, some offerings enable administrators to develop a global object schema across these data sources, defining their own types and functions and applying these to various back-end products.

These technologies are still relatively new, but they represent an important development in the universal DBMS arena. They demonstrate that many of the object/relational extensions we've discussed in earlier chapters can be linked into "legacy" environments. Doing so offers firms the potential to leverage universal DBMS technology in IT architectures where data is distributed across a network and likely to remain so.

We've seen how file links and virtual databases can help firms apply universal DBMS technology to remote data.

They can help universal DBMSs coexist with and bring added value to existing environments.

CHAPTER 10

Alternatives to Universal DBMSs

In the past nine chapters, we've explored in some detail the potential business value and feature set of universal DBMSs. We've seen how relational technology is being extended to support object-oriented concepts. And we've explored how these extensions may ripple through the DBMS itself in order to provide firms with extensibility as well as reasonable levels of performance.

But there are other approaches to supporting the "universe" of data types and a wide range of applications. We'll explore several major alternatives in this chapter.

Some vendors have taken different approaches to supporting new data types and new applications.

Overview

Our working definition of a universal DBMS—first introduced in Chapter 2—has been one that supports custom data types and query functions without requiring separate server processes, separate administrative facilities, and separate application programming interfaces (APIs). Our definition has also presumed an existing relational base extended in various ways to support object-oriented concepts and cope with performance issues.

Admittedly, this definition is somewhat arbitrary. For example, it's possible to build a new universal DBMS from scratch, without using existing code from a relational DBMS. Indeed, the first object/relational offerings—originally marketed as hybrid DBMSs or unified DBMSs—did just that. These revolutionary products captured considerable market interest but failed to reach wide deployment for a variety of reasons. Firms were unwilling to entrust critical corporate data to a brand-new DBMS produced by a small vendor. Integration with existing systems was difficult. And companies worried about code quality, system management difficulty, lack of third-party tools, and other issues.

Today, the industry has turned its attention to activities of larger vendors pursuing a universal DBMS strategy or a reasonable alternative. There's still no precise, "standard" definition of what exactly a universal DBMS is. So the previous chapters of this book simply used one common interpretation.

We'll investigate four broad alternatives to universal DBMSs.

But it's time to consider other ways in which DBMS extensibility can be achieved. Indeed, some products that employ rather different architectures are occasionally marketed as universal DBMSs. Other approaches to managing a wide range of data types and integrating object technology include

- object DBMSs
- object mapping services for a relational DBMS
- specialized database servers with an integration layer
- component-based software

We'll compare and contrast these alternatives with the stricter definition of a universal DBMS presented throughout this book.

Object DBMSs

In the late 1980s through early 1990s, a number of small vendors released new DBMS products that were not based on the relational approach. These products were *object* DBMSs and borrowed heavily from object-oriented programming languages (typically, C++) in an attempt to provide a more flexible environment than the relational DBMSs available at that time.

Object DBMSs integrate tightly with object-oriented programming languages to provide extensibility.

These object DBMSs were revolutionary in that they were built from scratch with a different code base and a different data model. Features included support for multiple data structures (tabular and nontabular), classes or types of objects that were user-defined, close integration with C++ or another object-oriented programming language, and a navigational approach to data access. Value-based queries—a hallmark of relational DBMSs—often weren't supported or were quite restrictive. Object DBMSs maintain these characteristics today, although query support has improved over initial releases.

Object DBMS vendors first established themselves in certain niches that weren't well supported by relational products. For example, computer-aided design applications were an early target market. Such applications had to work with complex, highly interrelated data structures—perhaps understanding how various components of an airplane engine or computer chip interface to one another. Much of this data couldn't be represented efficiently in the rows and columns of simple tables using simple data types like character strings and numbers. And since some of these new applications were being written in object-oriented programming languages, the use of an object DBMS provided a more familiar, seamless environment than a relational DBMS.

Their early design objectives were quite different from relational DBMSs.

Initial Product Differences

	Object DBMS	Relational DBMS
Data types	User-defined	Numeric, alphanumeric
Data structure	User-defined	Tabular
Programming languages	Object-oriented (C++, Smalltalk)	Many (C, COBOL, Fortran, 4GLs, etc.)
Data access	Navigational	Value- or query-based

Some thought they'd signal the demise of relational products.

Early success in certain market areas prompted some individuals in the IT industry to tout object DBMSs as the obvious replacement for relational DBMSs—the "next wave" in database management.

But that didn't really happen.

But that wave didn't sweep broadly across the shores of industry. Firms found early releases of object DBMSs lacking the same level of reliability, availability, and scalability they had found in relational DBMSs. Integration with C++ or Smalltalk didn't help if most of your applications were written in COBOL or your programmers were accustomed to working with a fourth-generation language. And the performance strengths that object DBMSs demonstrated for certain types of applications (such as those in the engineering field) often didn't translate well into the typical applications run by many firms. Limited administrative facilities, comparatively poor support for ad hoc query and report writing, and the challenges of integrating a new DBMS into existing IT environments were some of the factors that inhibited the success of object DBMSs.

More than a decade after their market debut, object DBMSs have improved considerably since their early releases. Yet these products have not enjoyed the same level of financial success and market acceptance as their relational DBMS counterparts did within their initial 10-year period. Although their use has grown, object DBMSs have not become the successor to relational DBMSs. Some question, however, whether object DBMSs might not provide a better approach to solving many of the problems that universal DBMSs are attempting to address.

Publicity surrounding universal DBMSs has caused some to revisit object DBMSs.

Among other things, today's object DBMSs provide *persistence* to objects created in languages such as C++, Java, and Smalltalk. Programmers define new types or classes of objects in these languages (employing any data structure they care to code) and create instances of these objects. Using mechanisms provided by an object DBMS, programmers can cause these instances to be stored and shared with others.

Object DBMSs support any classes and data structures that firms care to code.

Thus, object DBMSs can be highly flexible, supporting a wide range of structures and types. In effect, they can be thought of as an extension of an object-oriented programming environment, since integration with the programming language is nearly seamless. This differs from relational and universal DBMS approaches, which introduce a separate API (based on SQL) to work with stored data. Furthermore, object-oriented programmers don't need to map their class definitions into data types supported by the DBMS, as they do with relational or universal DBMSs. However, there's a downside to this approach, in that data independence can be much more difficult to achieve.

No one needs to translate the "object" view to the "DBMS" view.

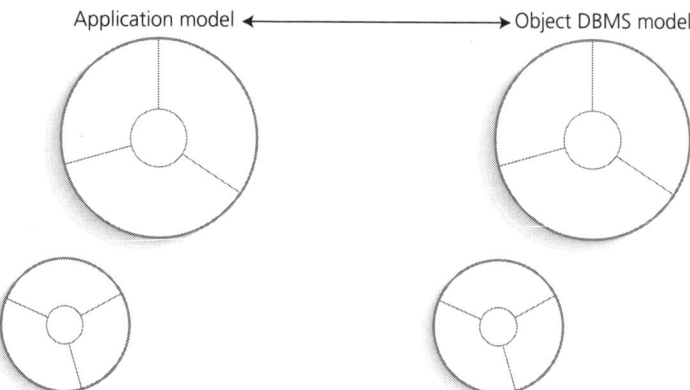

Their design is typically client-centric and presumes navigational access.

Object DBMSs often feature a highly client-centric architecture, managing a cache of objects on the client machine and providing a quick means to navigate through interrelated objects. This architecture is highly suitable for certain applications, such as iterative design work. However, for applications in which support for many concurrent ad hoc queries is important, a server-centric approach typically fares better.

Here are some of the reasons why firms tend to consider object DBMSs.

Object DBMSs tend to be considered by firms that

- want seamless integration with a specific object-oriented programming language
- prefer a navigational approach to data access and have little (if any) need to query stored data in an ad hoc manner
- expect to work frequently with complex user-defined types and user-defined storage structures, most of which will not be tabular in nature

- expect to build applications in which iterative access to a given set of objects is common, and high performance for these applications is needed

- require tools designed primarily for professional object-oriented programmers (tools and ready-made applications for novice users are not required or are a lower priority)

- have evaluated relational and/or universal DBMS offerings and find these to be lacking for some reason

If you're getting the impression that object DBMSs are fundamentally different from relational DBMSs and universal DBMSs, you're right. While both object DBMSs and universal DBMSs provide firms with an extensible environment, they achieve this in different ways and have some fundamentally different design points.

Such products are quite different from relational products.

The next three options are evolutionary approaches built on or otherwise encompassing existing relational DBMSs.

Object/Relational Mapping Services

A second alternative to universal DBMSs is less dramatic and arguably less costly for a DBMS vendor or a third party to build. It calls for an object services layer to be built *on top of* a relational DBMS. Thus, the DBMS itself is left unchanged. An external layer of code simulates an object-oriented environment, presumably enabling programmers to work with complex structures and types while storing their objects (really, just the data elements) in simple tables using a predefined set of data types.

Another approach calls for firms to map their objects to a relational DBMS.

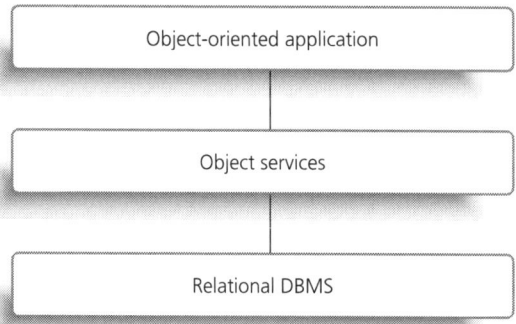

A separate layer helps facilitate this, often providing simple *1:1* mappings (1 class to 1 table) automatically. More complex mappings may also be supported.

Some relational DBMS vendors initially supported this approach.

Indeed, after object DBMSs hit the market, some relational DBMS vendors responded by tactically supporting independent offerings that provided object/relational translation services. Such offerings typically consisted of C++ class libraries and (sometimes) administrative facilities. A number of these offerings still exist and are relatively inexpensive to purchase. More recent offerings offer performance enhancements—such as a shareable object cache, usually located on an application server—that can minimize overhead and support iterative access in a more efficient manner. Java support is also available from a number of vendors. In addition to these ready-made solutions, some firms have built their own object services class libraries for the relational DBMS of their choice.

Here's why firms typically consider these mapping services.

In general, the object/relational mapping approach often appeals to firms that

- have made a strategic commitment to object-oriented development for new applications
- already have relational DBMSs in house
- require strong ad hoc query support

- require a wide range of ready-made tools and applications for their DBMS
- are conservative by nature, seeking to minimize risk by introducing object-oriented technology slowly into their enterprise

An obvious question arises: Why don't such firms migrate to a universal DBMS or upgrade their relational DBMS to the latest "universal" release?

The reasons for this vary. But release upgrades can be costly, both in software charges and in labor. Object/relational technology is still new and relatively untested in production environments; many firms prefer not to be on the "bleeding edge." Their existing (relational) DBMSs work. Instead of fixing something that isn't broken, why not just focus on interfacing new object-oriented applications to a proven product/release?

These are valid business considerations. Unfortunately, there's more to be considered. The process of mapping data from an object model into a relational model can be tedious and difficult, requiring complex structures to be "flattened" in some way and attributes of new data types to be mapped into the simpler type system supported by the target DBMS. While some commercial products provide automatic object/relational mapping services, they can't be optimized for every possible case. As a practical matter, a programmer or administrator often needs to get involved to fine-tune the mapping and cope with complex issues. This can be labor-intensive.

But mapping complex object structures into a relational DBMS can be tough.

But there are bigger issues beyond mapping from one model to another. Among these is performance. Because the underlying relational DBMS is unchanged, features such as new access methods or user-defined optimization extensions aren't present. This forces any data type-specific performance enhancements to be implemented outside the DBMS, either in applications or in the object/relational

Performance is also an issue.

mapping layer. Architecturally, neither approach provides the same performance advantage as integrating enhancements inside the engine itself.

Finally, most commercial offerings are supported by relatively small vendors. Some firms are reluctant to depend on smaller vendors for critical business applications, fearing that technical support may be weak or the longevity of the firm may be questionable. Such business issues also deserve some consideration and should be discussed with the appropriate vendor(s).

Specialized Servers with an Integration Layer

A third approach involves several specialized servers.

A third option to supporting a wide range of data types and functions involves the use of several specialized servers "glued" together by an integration layer. In this scenario, the integration layer presents programmers with a unified view of different data server processes, each of which is tailored toward supporting a specific set of data types and functions.

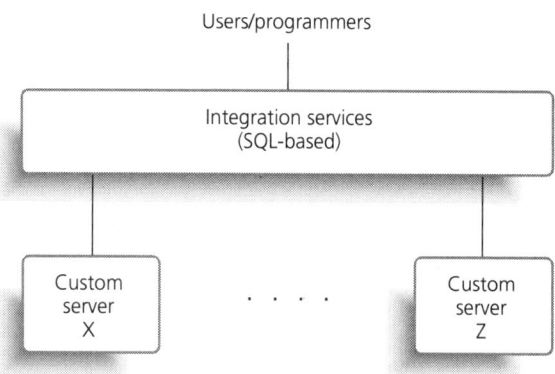

These are linked together by an integration layer to provide firms with a unified view of their data.

Thus, an environment might include a traditional relational DBMS server, a specialized text server, a specialized geo-spatial server, a specialized image server, and so on. A primary argument in favor of this approach is that each server can be tailored to provide the specific features and functions necessary for its target market. Some argue that this is easier—and more practical—to build than a "one-size-fits-all" system that needs to be extensible enough to accommodate existing and future business needs.

However, it's important to realize that vendors supporting this approach may not allow just any server to plug into their architecture. Don't assume that this option enables you to select your favorite relational DBMS from vendor X, your favorite text server from vendor Y, and your favorite geo-spatial engine from vendor Z and perceive these as one integrated environment. Instead, it's more common that your DBMS vendor will have a suite of separately priced server products that can be linked together to simulate a unified system.

Usually, only the servers supported by a single vendor can participate in this environment.

Some firms find this appealing, as it avoids finger-pointing when problems occur and can even offer a strong position from which to negotiate terms and conditions for software and support. Others dislike the dependency on a single vendor, particularly if support of a needed suite of data types and functions is limited or nonexistent.

That has both advantages and disadvantages.

In general, companies that favor this approach

■ require a limited number of new data types and functions beyond those already supported by relational DBMSs

■ require strong ad hoc query support but often don't need to write single queries that "touch" several different forms of non-traditional data

Here's why this approach appeals to some firms.

- can support a database design in which specialized data is largely segregated
- don't mind making a strategic commitment to one particular DBMS vendor for critical business applications
- don't have a desire to define new data types, new functions, new access methods, and the like (a ready-made approach is preferred)
- are somewhat conservative by nature

As we mentioned, this approach has some drawbacks. Indeed, critics argue that this approach fails to meet a primary objective of universal data management: extensibility. Although the overall environment can accommodate a wide range of data types and functions, it may provide for limited extensibility by third parties. Firms may not be able to define new, complex types. Defining or extending existing access methods may not be supported. And other object/relational features discussed earlier in this book may not be present.

Performance, overall function, and administrative issues need to be considered.

Performance, function, and system management also warrant consideration. To what extent can the integration layer effectively break down multiserver queries and devise a reasonable data access strategy? What specialized access methods and optimization functions are provided for each server? What restrictions, if any, are placed on the number of servers that can be referenced in a single query? Are new utilities and system management tools required for each new server? Can integrity constraints span servers? How can backup/recovery operations be coordinated across servers? How can problem diagnosis and performance tuning be supported across servers?

Component-Based Software

A final approach we'll consider calls for data sources to be perceived as object-oriented *components* that all support a common set of object-oriented interfaces. These data sources may be relational DBMSs, spreadsheets, email systems, file systems, or a variety of others. Thus, the component-based approach can be thought of as supporting the "universe" of data types and applications. Perhaps the most well-known supporter of this approach is Microsoft, although other vendors have proposed or implemented other component-based architectures. For our discussion, we'll draw largely on Microsoft's OLE DB approach as an example.

A fourth approach allows programmers to perceive different data sources as "components" with a common object-oriented interface.

Extensibility is provided by enabling any data source vendor to write the code necessary to conform to interface specifications. Although SQL data sources can be supported (via an ODBC component), the overall interface employed by this approach is not SQL-based. Instead, the interface is object-based. Each "object type" has a number of interfaces associated with it to provide users with necessary functions. Examples of object types include data sources, indexes, rowsets (conceptually similar to a tabular result set), transactions, and errors. Interfaces provide a means to learn how to query a particular data source, read from or write data to the data source, start a transaction, commit/abort a transaction, and so on.

A primary difference between this approach and the universal DBMS approach discussed throughout this book is that the component-based approach doesn't attempt to bring new forms of data within a single DBMS. Instead, data remains in its native formats, possibly on remote systems. Rather than *managing* the "universe" of data, this approach focuses on providing universal *access* to this data. Programmers perceive each data source to be a component that conforms to a minimal common set of interfaces, presenting data to requesting applications in a tabular format.

Data continues to exist in its native formats and is not moved into a single DBMS.

A publicly available specification enables data providers to write code to plug into this scheme.

In some respects, this approach is similar to having specialized servers with an integration layer. However, the integration layer here is fairly thin. Indeed, it is really a *specification* for how data source providers can "plug into" this scheme. Second, the component-based approach is designed to support a wider range of data sources built by third parties, including many data sources contained in popular desktop software packages that are not relational. Third, applications don't need to use SQL. Rather, this approach specifies a set of several dozen interfaces associated with a small number of components (or object types). C and C++ programmers can use these fundamental interfaces. An optional software layer allows higher-level access to these data components from Visual Basic, Java, and other languages.

In other respects, the component-based approach is similar to the multidatabase server software discussed in Chapter 9. However, multidatabase servers may contain all or part of a relational or object/relational DBMS engine within them, providing for local storage of data and global optimization of data access. Furthermore, multidatabase servers typically rely on an SQL interface, providing little (if any) access to desktop data sources such as email systems, spreadsheets, or project management software.

This approach saves data movement costs but potentially increases data management complexity.

It's still too early to tell how successful the component-based approach to supporting the "universe" of data will be. Some argue that it avoids the need to move large amounts of data into a single data source—a potentially expensive proposition, and one that eliminates the use of many popular tools that don't employ SQL or tabular data structures. Others argue that the component-based approach introduces more data management complexity because the data resides in different sources and certain administrative functions, such as coordinated backups and recovery, aren't built in. Furthermore, the most widely discussed component-based approach is backed largely by a single vendor. To be successful, a large number of data providers (vendors who produce software that stores data) will have to comply with the specification.

In general, firms consider this approach when they

> **Here's why firms tend to consider this approach.**

- have a reasonable amount of existing data in relational and nonrelational data sources, particularly those used by popular desktop packages or LAN server software (these might include email systems, spreadsheets, word processors, etc.)
- want to provide programmers with simplified access to these disparate data sources in a uniform manner (and achieving this access without surfacing an SQL interface is acceptable or desirable)
- want to avoid copying or migrating data from a given data source into a single data source, such as a universal DBMS
- don't mind basing all or part of their data access strategy on a specification that is largely supported by one major vendor
- find that desired data sources already conform to this approach or are expected to do so soon

Summary

We've looked at four broad alternatives to universal DBMSs (or at least the working definition of universal DBMS that we've been using throughout this book). Object DBMSs were the first to debut, and their appearance predated that of universal DBMSs. Object DBMSs are revolutionary products, in that they call for new systems to be built from scratch based upon an object data model. This data model, although not as precisely defined as the relational data model, generally leverages object-oriented programming language concepts quite heavily and presumes a data access approach that is largely navigational.

> **We've seen that universal DBMSs aren't the only way to support varied data types and applications.**

Other options include object DBMSs, mapping services, special servers with an integration layer, and component-based software.

Shortly after object DBMSs became available, early commercial offerings of object/relational mapping services also appeared. These products enable firms to use existing relational DBMSs and simulate an object-oriented interface to programmers. Object class definitions are mapped to relational tables in some fashion, and programmers can use methods provided by the object/relational service layer to cause relational DBMS activities to occur (such as inserting new rows into a table or retrieving data from a table). If desired, programmers can employ SQL themselves in many cases. Thus, object/relational mapping services are an evolutionary approach.

A more recent approach—sometimes marketed as a universal DBMS—involves using specialized servers to support select data types and functions. These servers are lashed together by an integration layer, which presents a unified environment to programmers. One of these servers may be a traditional relational DBMS, so this approach can be thought of as evolutionary as well. Restrictions generally apply regarding the types of data servers supported and the number of servers that can be referenced in a single query.

Finally, at least one major vendor is supporting the notion of universal data access rather than a universal DBMS. Data sources (including DBMSs, file systems, email systems, etc.) are perceived as components that share a common interface that is not SQL-based. Each data source maintains its own data but provides generalized access. The success of this approach depends, in part, on the willingness of data providers to conform to this specification and the ease in which the overall environment can be managed.

As you might imagine, each of these approaches has advantages and disadvantages relative to universal DBMSs. It's important to understand *your* unique DBMS requirements when evaluating options.

form
CHAPTER 11

What's the Bottom Line?

We've covered a lot of material so far. Hopefully, you now have a good idea of what universal database management is all about, how the technology can be applied to environments in which data is physically distributed, and what some of the major alternatives to this technology are. It's worthwhile to step back and summarize some of the major benefits commonly associated with universal DBMSs. And in the interest of providing a more balanced perspective, we should consider some of the common criticisms levied against these products. Finally, we'll consider future trends that are likely to impact this technology area.

Let's step back and weigh the benefits of universal DBMSs against some of the common criticisms. Then we can speculate about the future.

Business Benefits

Still relatively new to the market, firms are buying and deploying universal DBMSs because they expect to realize certain business benefits by doing so. We've already touched on a number of these potential benefits in previous chapters when we explored specific features and functions associated with universal DBMSs. We'll revisit the topic again here, now that you have a better overall understanding of the technology.

Universal DBMSs are still rather new.

But we can see how they can minimize the need for specialized systems.

Improved support for real-world data types and complex structures is a major goal of universal DBMSs. We've already seen examples of how critical business data doesn't just consist of simple character strings and numbers. Enabling many forms of data to be effectively managed by a single DBMS can minimize the need to purchase and maintain separate file systems or specialized data servers. This can potentially lead to reduced software cost. Savings in labor are also possible, as some system integration and maintenance issues will be minimized.

They also allow critical data to be analyzed and leveraged in new ways.

Of course, integrated support for new data types can facilitate new forms of data analysis. A simple example involves geographic analysis, which allows the locations of certain business objects—customers, distribution centers, suppliers, and so on—to be factored into a key decision. But universal DBMSs don't require that new analytic capabilities exist separately from traditional ones. Indeed, the whole idea is to enable firms to combine traditional SQL capabilities with new, user-defined functions to enable their staff to leverage existing data in new ways.

Presumably, better business decisions will result.

Trying to quantify the value of enabling new forms of analysis is elusive, but presumably new analytic capabilities contribute to improved business decisions. Furthermore, support for new data types and new forms of analysis can enable firms to create applications that weren't practical to build before.

Greater code reuse and improved data integrity are other potential benefits.

Code reuse, reduced application maintenance, and enhanced data integrity are other potential benefits. By enabling firms to push many of their data-oriented business rules down into the DBMS, universal offerings eliminate the need to hard-code these rules into all the necessary applications. Furthermore, the DBMS will automatically enforce these rules, preventing inadvertent violations from occurring that could compromise the integrity of the data. Other mechanisms, such as strong typing for user-defined data types, also contribute to data integrity and help ensure that nonsensical or misleading operations won't be performed.

Finally, greater synergy with object-oriented programming concepts is also a feature of universal DBMSs. For firms committed to object-oriented design and development, this can be important as some of the "impedance mismatch" evident between object-oriented programming languages and relational DBMSs is eliminated. Again, this offers potential savings in labor costs, as firms are likely to have a less difficult time mapping the "object" view of the world to the "DBMS" view of the world. Some performance benefits may also result because of internal DBMS extensions (primarily in the area of indexing and optimization) as well as new database design options.

And there's a greater synergy with object-oriented programming.

While these aren't the only potential benefits associated with universal DBMSs, they're some of the most commonly discussed. Yet universal DBMSs are far from perfect, and not everyone is convinced they're the ideal approach. (Indeed, the previous chapter discussed four alternatives.) Let's take some time, then, to consider some of the criticisms of these products.

Of course, this is just a partial list. But you get the idea.

Common Criticisms

Criticisms of universal DBMSs can be divided into two broad categories: business issues and technical issues. On the business side, universal DBMSs are still rather new and not widely deployed as of this writing. This leads to concerns about scalability and performance in production environments, as well as staffing difficulties. As we've seen, universal DBMSs introduce a number of new functions that affect database design and system administration. Finding skilled staff in this area is likely to be tough, and building up these skills in-house

Nonetheless, these products aren't perfect.

They require time to learn.

What's the Bottom Line?

requires time and an investment in training. In addition, locating a wide range of third-party tools that exploit new universal DBMS functions can also be challenging.

And vendor hype can make product selection quite difficult.

Moreover, the universal DBMS market is still somewhat fragmented. Some DBMS firms are pursuing the universal approach described in this book, while others are pursuing one of the alternatives described in the previous chapter or taking a "wait-and-see" attitude. To further confuse the issue, products that possess considerably different features (and sometimes fundamentally different architectures) are often all marketed as "universal" offerings. As a result, some businesses—particularly those that are more conservative by nature—are approaching the universal DBMS market with caution.

Some people question if it's wise to try to build a single DBMS to manage the "universe" of data types.

Of course, there are technical criticisms of the universal DBMS approach as well. Some believe it's impractical to build a "one-size-fits-all" DBMS, arguing that performance is likely to suffer and the complexity of doing so is too great. Others argue that expecting firms to migrate or copy data into a single DBMS is unrealistic, too expensive, and simply inefficient. Specialized servers with an integration layer and component-based software are usually offered as more effective alternatives.

And integration with object-oriented programming languages isn't seamless.

In addition, some enthusiasts of object-oriented technology question the viability of an object/relational approach. After all, universal DBMSs still maintain their own data type system and require the use of a separate application programming interface (API). While the type system and API of universal DBMSs are more flexible and extensible than those of traditional relational DBMSs, they still don't provide for a seamless integration with an object-oriented programming language. Thus, some type mapping still needs to occur, and application developers still need to work with SQL.

Even those who aren't ardent supporters of a "pure" object model have raised concerns about the direction being taken by the SQL3 standards effort on object/relational technology. As of this writing, efforts aren't finalized but are generally stable in many key areas. And many of these areas are already provoking criticism. Support for denormalized tables, the introduction of references, the apparent incongruities of certain new features, and some of the proposed syntax have elicited concern from consultants and third parties.

SQL standards efforts are still evolving, but some aspects have caused concern.

Finally, leveraging many of the features of a universal DBMS is no trivial matter. Consider the options for defining new data types and working these types into a new database design. Relatively little information is available to date to guide firms through this design process, which is likely to force some IT professionals to adopt a trial-and-error approach in the short term. And if we expand the task to include not just data type and table definitions but the introduction of new functions and new performance enhancements, the job gets tougher quickly. In some implementations, a further complexity is introduced because complementary DBMS tools and utilities may provide limited support for some of the newer universal DBMS functions.

Database design is likely to be tricky, particularly at first.

And tools support may be lacking.

Future Trends

All this begs the question: what does the future hold for universal DBMSs? Many industry analysts and consultants are mildly optimistic to quite enthusiastic about the long-range potential for universal DBMSs, largely because they perceive such products as helping to solve a common set of business problems. And many of the major DBMS vendors are investing heavily in this technology, convinced that it will enable them to bring added value to existing customers as well as elicit new business.

Yet many analysts are generally upbeat about the future of universal DBMSs.

So, from a business point of view, it's quite likely that IT professionals at medium- to large-sized firms will have an opportunity to work with some form of a universal DBMS now or in the near future. From a technical standpoint, universal DBMSs are still in their early days and will continue to be refined for some time.

Watch for performance and system management improvements.

Performance improvements are likely to be one area of emphasis, with support for additional optimization enhancements, improved resource utilization, and parallel processing likely to surface. Enhancements in the areas of systems management, DBMS utilities, system tuning, and diagnostics are likely to be others.

Good application development tools will also be critical.

But the technical challenges extend beyond the DBMS engine itself. Indeed, a primary challenge involves effective support of object-oriented application development. What can be done to bridge the gap between classes designed in C++, Java, Smalltalk, or IDL and the extensible type systems supported by universal DBMSs? Will there be a reasonable way to push down the invocation of appropriate methods into the DBMS, given the existence of user-defined functions? Will programmers be able to cache certain DBMS objects on the client tier or a middle tier to improve performance for particular applications? While universal DBMSs provide additional mechanisms that help firms overcome the impedance mismatch with object-oriented programming languages, new tools need to be developed to automate and support this. Some vendors have begun working on these issues, but much remains to be done.

And other complementary products need to be enhanced to exploit new universal DBMS functions.

And, as we've already mentioned, other DBMS tools need to be extended as well to exploit new functions. For example, graphics-based query/report writing tools may need to move beyond the familiar icons, pop-up windows, and menu items to provide a more intuitive way to formulate geographic-oriented queries. Data replication facilities must cope with the new data types and structures introduced by universal DBMSs, and doing so in a mixed-vendor environment can be particularly challenging. Ready-made applications for vertical markets (such as finance, manufacturing, etc.) may also benefit by capitalizing on new universal DBMS features.

Summary

Potential business benefits of universal DBMSs stem from functions that provide integrated support for new types of data, enable new forms of business analysis to be performed on that data, and provide for automatic enforcement of many key business rules. Cost savings, code reuse, and a more integrated IT environment may all result in time.

Universal DBMSs promise to bring firms a number of benefits.

But current offerings aren't perfect. Critics argue that some are still difficult to use and largely unproven in production environments. Others question the merits of certain functions, dislike the continued reliance on SQL, and become concerned about the relatively small number of third-party tools designed to exploit universal DBMS features rather than tolerate them (or ignore them).

We're still in the early days, and there's more work to be done.

Despite this, many IT analysts are optimistic about the future of universal DBMSs, although they expect broad deployment to take time and require additional technical improvements, including greater performance enhancements and improved systems management capabilities. A robust suite of tools—particularly those that support effective object-oriented application development—are also needed to round out the efforts of universal DBMS vendors.

But leading analysts and vendors are optimistic about the future.

CHAPTER 12

Is Universal Database Management Right for You?

Now that you're familiar with universal database management, perhaps you're wondering if this technology might be right for you. This chapter provides some guidelines in that respect. These guidelines are designed to help you evaluate if you might require universal DBMS technology and, if so, how you might go about assessing different vendors' implementations. Finally, we'll also discuss some of the issues you should consider *before* deploying any universal DBMS solution.

While universal DBMSs may sound exciting, how can you determine if they're what you need?

Evaluation Guidelines

While many of the features associated with universal DBMSs sound appealing, getting caught up in the allure of any new technology seldom leads to a wise business decision. It's best to step back and review your business requirements and IT challenges to evaluate if universal DBMSs may really be of use to your firm. We'll discuss both technical and business considerations to keep in mind. The issues presented here are by no means exhaustive, but should provide a reasonable starting point.

Here are some questions to ask yourself—and universal DBMS vendors.

Types of Data to Be Managed

Consider universal DBMSs if you need a rich, extensible data type system.

A major area in which universal DBMSs differ from more traditional systems is their data type support. Therefore, such products can be useful if you need to

- manage "unusual" or specialized data types, including geographic data, time series data, and various forms of multimedia data
- model complex data that has its own internal structure
- capture the semantics associated with simple or complex data types
- leverage certain object-oriented concepts and provide for greater synergy with object-oriented applications

Compare vendor offerings closely.

Although a number of vendors offer some level of support for user-defined data types, implementations do differ. This book used proposed SQL3 syntax to illustrate how new data types may be created and used, but there are other approaches. When comparing vendor offerings, investigate the following:

- Any restrictions associated with type creation. For example, can both simple and complex types be defined to the DBMS? Can complex types be used in either table or column definitions?

- Any restrictions associated with how data types are used. For example, if you expect to create tables with columns defined as large objects, consider any limitations associated with writing queries, loading data, or performing other functions that involve large object data.

Pay attention to restrictions and coding requirements associated with new data types.

- The coding requirements for creating new data types. Is it all SQL-based, or does some code need to be written in a programming language such as C?

- Support for strong typing. In general, strongly typed implementations are preferable to weakly typed implementations, as strong typing provides added integrity and helps prevent nonsensical operations from occurring.
- Support for hierarchies and inheritance. Such features provide for incremental refinement and can promote code reuse. If you expect to use table hierarchies, understand physical storage options and how these might affect performance for your queries.

Business Rules to Be Enforced

Universal DBMSs also feature a number of mechanisms that provide for a more "active" overall environment—an environment in which the system can take action automatically to enforce certain business rules. While traditional DBMSs also provide some support for this, universal DBMSs typically attempt to do more. Furthermore, universal DBMSs often enable firms to create new functions to facilitate new types of queries.

Consider a universal DBMS if you

- have a reasonable number of specific business rules or policies the DBMS should automatically enforce
- need to initiate non-DBMS activities whenever certain changes to a user database occur
- want to develop new functions to simplify the work of certain applications or make new forms of data analysis more practical
- want to push some application logic closer to the DBMS to facilitate code reuse and/or realize potential performance gains

Look to a universal DBMS if you need a more "active" overall environment.

Compare vendor implementations of triggers, event alerters, user-defined SQL functions, and stored procedures.

A number of universal DBMSs—and some relational DBMSs—support one or more features that make for a more active overall environment, promote code reuse, and extend the expressiveness of SQL. These features, which we discussed in Chapter 5, include CHECK constraints, triggers, event alerters, user-defined functions, and stored procedures. Since some of these features were offered first in "traditional" relational DBMSs, implementations vary quite a bit. When evaluating vendor support in this area, try to understand the following:

Ask about coding requirements and system management issues.

- Coding requirements for triggers, event alerters, user-defined functions, and stored procedures. Are these written in a specific SQL dialect, a third-generation programming language, or some combination of the two? What mechanisms, if any, are provided for exception handling and debugging? If programming languages can be used, which are supported?

- Storage and management issues of event alerters, user-defined functions, and stored procedures. Do these reside within or outside the user database? In either case, can they be considered part of standard maintenance operations, such as database backup and recovery?

- Restrictions associated with the number and types of triggers supported per table. If multiple triggers of the same type are permitted on a given column of a table, can an administrator control the order in which each will be executed? If nested trigger execution is supported, can an administrator disable such support or control the degree of nesting?

- Execution options for user-defined functions. Can an administrator control where the function will be run (in the DBMS address space or a separate address space)?

Performance Issues

Performance is typically a key concern associated with any DBMS. And since universal DBMSs are still relatively new, little comparative benchmark data is available. However, such systems generally aim to support ad hoc query (or value-based) access over a mixture of simple and complex data types. Although some navigational access is supported, creating an environment in which programmers can quickly follow pointers or a chain of linked records isn't the primary design goal of most universal DBMSs. Therefore, the performance metric that should be used to evaluate universal DBMSs involves complex queries over varied forms of critical business data.

Universal DBMSs are designed to support query-based access over a combination of simple and complex data types.

What's available to help firms assess performance of universal DBMSs? Not much. But since many universal DBMSs are enhanced versions of a relational DBMS (or perhaps a merger of a relational DBMS code base and a newer code base), people are occasionally tempted to consult published benchmark data for relational products. Unfortunately, this won't reveal much about how a given universal DBMS might perform when it must manage a wider range of data types (many of which are user-defined) and support complex queries involving these types (including those that incorporate user-defined functions).

But don't expect to find many published benchmarks specific to universal DBMS functions.

Of course, you could install and test multiple universal DBMSs using your own data and your own workload. Indeed, this would give you the most accurate performance information. But not every firm is willing to undertake such an effort. A second alternative—admittedly one that is less conclusive—involves evaluating features that can contribute to improved performance. These include the following:

Instead, look for built-in features that can influence performance.

Monitoring and tuning facilities, optimization extensions, and new indexing mechanisms are all areas to investigate.

- Performance monitoring and tuning facilities. You'll probably want the same minimal set generally supported for relational DBMSs, particularly a facility for viewing the data access plan selected by the optimizer and a means to monitor resource utilization.

- Mechanisms to "educate" or influence the optimizer. Are users or programmers expected to provide data access directives in their queries or applications? Are programmers who create new functions expected to include optimization guidelines as part of their function definitions and/or update associated catalog statistics?

- Indexing extensions. Can new access methods be introduced? If so, to what level are they integrated within the DBMS? What are the coding requirements associated with supported indexing extensions? Can the output of functions be indexed?

- Special handling of large objects, if you plan to use these. Memory management, logging, and storage options are all important considerations associated with these data types.

Complementary Tools and Class Libraries

Also assess the tools available for end users, programmers, and system administrators.

Few firms purchase DBMSs without any consideration about available tools and applications. If you're thinking about deploying a universal DBMS in a production environment, you probably want to understand what supporting products are available for the DBMSs you're evaluating. The following areas are worth investigating:

- Query/report writing, application development, and system management offerings. Are they available only from the DBMS vendor or from a variety of popular independent software vendors? What unique universal DBMS features do these tools exploit, or do available offerings merely tolerate the DBMS, perhaps working with it as a generic relational DBMS?

- Ready-made class libraries. Are offerings available to support the data types and functions you need? If the class libraries you need are offered by third parties, were they subjected to a certification process or built as part of a joint effort with the DBMS vendor? Did the third parties take advantage of DBMS performance features, perhaps introducing new access methods and/or optimization enhancements? How will technical support and service be handled?

Lean toward buying class libraries, unless you can afford the extra development effort.

Standards Compliance and "Openness"

Questions about standards compliance and the overall "openness" of a software offering often are raised in the early days of any new technology. Such questions typically stem from concerns about vendor lock-in and a need to minimize the risk of deploying a solution that may be rendered obsolete by a shift in the IT industry.

Consider a universal DBMS if your initial platform requirements involve one of the popular UNIX platforms or Windows NT, since most offerings are targeting these platforms initially. An OS/390 implementation is expected from at least one major vendor. Since the SQL3 standards are not finalized as of this writing, balance the importance of standards compliance with your need to deploy a viable solution in the short term. If you decide to implement a universal DBMS solution before all your required SQL capabilities have been standardized, minimize your risk by selecting a DBMS vendor that is active in the SQL standards effort and has publicly committed to compliance.

Most universal DBMSs run on UNIX or Windows NT. Some are expected to follow emerging industry standards.

Integration with Existing IT Systems

Determine if your universal DBMS will need to import existing data, connect to external data sources, or integrate with Web technology. Then examine vendor support closely.

Introduction of a new DBMS—or a "universal" release of an existing relational DBMS—raises an integration issue. Chances are that the universal DBMS will need to fit into a broader IT architecture that encompasses more traditional DBMS products, a variety of file systems, and other data sources. Integration issues naturally become important.

When evaluating universal DBMSs from this perspective, try to understand the following:

- What facilities, if any, are available to help administrators import or migrate data from popular data sources into the universal DBMS environment? For example, if GIF images or Adobe files contain important corporate data, does the universal DBMS or a class library have the built-in ability to read these files and copy them into a user database?

- What facilities, if any, are available to allow external data sources to participate in a broad universal DBMS environment? For example, is file link technology available to enable local or remote files to be tied to user tables? Is some form of universal access to disparate and physically distributed data supported, perhaps via a multidatabase server, point-to-point gateways, or component-based technology?

- What synergy, if any, is provided between the DBMS and Web technology? With intranets becoming increasingly popular, and many firms offering customer-oriented Internet applications as well, the ability to use a Web browser to query and modify universal DBMS data is important to many firms. In some cases, the ability to manage Web content (such as HTML pages containing text, images, and Java applets) is an important DBMS function.

Other Issues

Of course, universal DBMSs need to be able to support fundamental database management functions, including high levels of availability, reliability, serviceability, security, and capacity. Again, because many universal DBMSs were built on a proven relational DBMS code base, they're able to capitalize on many years of refinement "for free." Understand the strengths and weaknesses of the underlying relational DBMS code base to develop some indication of potential problem areas. But watch for any significant restrictions associated with the newer universal functions described in this book, and try to contact other firms who've already used the technology to pinpoint potential problems early on.

And don't forget the basics of database management.

Consider also the vendor's stability and overall reputation in the industry. Is the vendor committed to universal DBMS technology and likely to be in a position to refine its offerings over time? What options are available for technical support, and what is the vendor's reputation in this area? Are consulting services and educational services available if needed? Are software quality problems generally fixed in a reasonable period of time? Is new product function generally delivered when promised? Are statements about strategic direction implemented in subsequent offerings?

Ask about available technical support services offered by different vendors.

Issues to Consider Before Deployment

If all this has left you convinced that a universal DBMS is in your future, it's probably time to consider what you can do to make sure your deployment is a success. This section is designed to give you some food for thought in that area. But again, use this information as a starting point for developing your own checklist of steps to take before implementing your solution.

Develop your own checklist of issues to address before you deploy a universal DBMS.

Staffing Issues

Allocate time for staff training. Try to identify people with prior DBMS and object-oriented skills.

If you want to exploit the extensibility of your universal DBMS, expect to invest in training for your staff. Individuals who've had prior relational DBMS experience and are familiar with object-oriented programming make good candidates for beginning a pilot project. Data modeling and database design experience are also important, especially if you expect to experiment with unconventional table structures and hierarchies (of both data types and tables). Consider limiting creation of new types and unusual table structures to a small set of individuals at first. Encourage these individuals to experiment with different ways of supporting your target applications so they can assess usability, system management, and performance issues under different circumstances.

Encourage your staff to network with peers at other firms.

If possible, allocate time for key individuals on your project to network with people at other companies who are using the product. This networking can include monitoring Usenet newsgroups, subscribing to technical mailing lists, scheduling periodic conference calls with interested parties, attending monthly or quarterly meetings hosted by local user groups, and initiating "birds of a feather" discussions at annual conferences. Connecting with others who've already been where you want to go can help you resolve problems more quickly and avoid costly mistakes.

IT Environmental Issues

Select your deployment platform carefully. Try to keep multi-tier environments as homogeneous as possible.

Most universal DBMSs run in client/server or multitier configurations. UNIX and NT platforms are most commonly supported, although at least one vendor is expected to offer an OS/390 implementation as well. It's important to ensure that the system administration staff has experience with the selected platforms and the networking software to be deployed. To minimize problems in the early stages, try to keep the IT environment as homogeneous as possible. If the same type of hardware and operating system can be used across all tiers, do so. Add other platforms later in the cycle, if needed.

Of course, you'll need to consider the number of concurrent users and the quantity of data you need to manage for capacity planning purposes. Ask your vendor about memory and disk space utilization issues *before* you make your final platform selection. Most vendors publish planning guidelines as part of their product library or education packages. Start with these, but try to sanity-check the information by networking with users of the product at other firms. And don't implement an unreasonably small workload as your test case. You need to get some idea of how the DBMS will perform under conditions that are typical in your organization.

Pay close attention to capacity planning issues. Try to implement a representative workload.

Finally, consider if connectivity to other data sources will be critical for your universal DBMS immediately or at some point in the future. If so, investigate alternatives offered by your vendor and third parties. Pay close attention to issues involving pricing, system management, performance, and data access restrictions because these can vary widely depending on the product in question. Plan for one phase of your project to focus on your required system integration issues, preferably after basic DBMS function has been tested and demonstrated to be effective.

Don't ignore system integration issues.

Target Applications

Selecting appropriate applications for your universal DBMS is important for both business and technical reasons. Assuming universal DBMS technology is new to your firm, select one to three applications as test cases for the product. Ideally, the applications you choose should be able to demonstrate clear business value to your firm and make use of a subset of key universal DBMS features. Don't try to build a single, mission-critical application that leverages every uni-

Pick a set of pilot projects carefully. Each should leverage a subset of key universal DBMS functions.

versal DBMS feature supported by your product. This will add considerable time (and risk) to the project. Instead, allow yourself time to test an important subset of functions and deliver a reasonable solution. Then build on that success by leveraging additional functions.

Get your application developers and database designers to collaborate on a schema.

If you expect to build new applications using an object-oriented programming language, plan to have your application programmer(s) and database designer(s) work together closely in the initial stages. As you've seen, universal DBMSs offer a number of functions to help ease the impedance mismatch between an application's view of the world and the DBMS's view of the world. But realizing this benefit isn't automatic. And balancing the needs of a set of applications with the desire to maintain a DBMS environment that provides for data independence can be quite challenging. Therefore, individuals involved in designing object-oriented classes and universal DBMS schemas must collaborate to avoid wasted time and effort.

Define specific measures to assess your project's success.

Before building your target applications, consider how you'll measure the success of your efforts. Ideally, such measurements should encompass not only functional and scheduling objectives, but also consider the return on investment that the technology has (or hasn't) brought to your firm. Quantified financial data is always desirable but often hard to come by. Minimally, however, you should be able to survey those who are using the new technology and determine if they feel more productive or effective in some way. While this may sound a bit bureaucratic, the extra effort can help you assess if it's really wise to deploy universal DBMS technology on a wider scale in your organization.

Summary

Although universal DBMSs introduce a number of compelling functions, they're not a silver bullet. In this chapter, we reviewed a variety of issues that can help you determine if a universal DBMS is right for you and, if so, how you might go about evaluating different commercial offerings. Unfortunately, products that bear the "universal" moniker often differ widely from one another. For the near term, then, you'll need to dig well beyond the marketing literature to determine which vendor's offering has the support you desire.

But selecting a universal DBMS is only one step along the road. There are a number of other business and technical issues you'll want to consider before you deploy your solution in order to ensure a reasonable chance of success. Again, this chapter offered some guidelines in that area.

With a number of the major DBMS vendors pursuing some sort of "universal" path, chances are you'll have the chance to work with one or more of these offerings in your career. If you're already familiar with relational DBMSs and object-oriented technology, you're off to a good start. Hopefully, this book has helped you understand how these two different disciplines are beginning to intersect and why a number of firms are already turning to universal DBMSs to support their new applications.

With many DBMS firms pursuing some "universal" strategy, you'll probably get a chance to work with such a system in the future.

Glossary

Abstract data type (ADT)
A specific form of a complex, user-defined data type. Abstract data types can be used when defining columns of a table or attributes of other abstract data types. They contain an internal structure, usually consisting of multiple attributes (or "fields").

Array
A type of **collection.** An ordered group of data values that may contain duplicates. Arrays have a predefined boundary (or length). Elements of an array may be accessed without starting at the beginning, and additional elements may be added anywhere within the array (not just at the end). See also **bag, list, set.**

Bag
A type of **collection.** An unordered group of data values that may contain duplicates. See also **array, list, set.**

B+-tree
An index structure commonly used by relational DBMSs (and universal DBMSs). B+-trees are balanced tree structures that can speed a variety of search operations, particularly those involving a range of key values.

Casting
The ability to treat values of one data type as though they were values of another data type for the purposes of some operation. For example, a simple user-defined data type for employee serial numbers may be temporarily cast as an integer to facilitate a comparison operation with the constant integer 1076.

Catalog

A set of tables within a relational or universal DBMS that contains *metadata,* or data about data. The catalog is necessary for DBMS operations. Among the data it contains is information about available tables, the number and types of columns for each table, the names and types of indexes defined on various tables, security permissions, and so on.

Class

A mechanism supported by object-oriented programming languages to enable programmers to define the attributes (data characteristics) and methods (valid functions or services) of new objects.

Class hierarchy

An object-oriented programming technique that enables programmers to derive new classes from existing classes, forming a hierarchic structure. Hierarchies and inheritance contribute to code reuse.

Class library

A package of ready-made software that usually consists of multiple classes designed to provide a useful set of services for object-oriented programmers. Universal DBMSs support conceptually similar libraries, which may consist of new data types, new functions, and new access methods. DBMS class libraries are available for supporting text data, geographic data, image data, data cleansing, and other areas.

Collection

A structure that typically contains a group of objects or data values. Universal DBMSs may support several kinds of collections, including **arrays, bags, lists,** and **sets.** Collections enable firms to define tables that have columns based on collections of various data types.

Complex data type
A user-defined data type that possesses its own internal structure. Complex types typically contain multiple attributes. These types can be used when defining a table, when defining columns of a table, or when defining attributes of other complex data types.

Constraint
An integrity rule specified when a table is created (or altered) to ensure input data falls within a valid data range. For example, a constraint on the SEX column of the EMPLOYEE table might ensure that only values of "M" or "F" are stored.

Constructor
A method that enables new instances of a class (new objects) to be created. With a universal DBMS, a constructor function is used to create a new instance of a complex data type that forms the basis of a column definition.

Database management system (DBMS)
Software that enables firms to effectively manage data. In this book, DBMSs are expected to support multiuser environments. This implies the need for functions that support backups, recovery, concurrency control, security, and other services.

Denormalized table
A tabular data structure that is not in first normal form. Such tables contain repeating groups. In other words, a column within a row may contain a collection or group of data values instead of a single data value. Such structures are not proper relations and are not permitted in a traditional relational DBMS. However, they are supported by some universal DBMSs.

Distinct type
A user-defined data type derived from a single, system-supplied data type. Distinct types are simple data types.

Encapsulation
An object-oriented programming technique that ensures that data elements of an object are accessed only through valid functions (or methods). In the universal DBMS arena, encapsulation can be supported through the use of complex data types. Associated functions (**constructors, mutators,** and **observers**) provide for encapsulation.

Event alerter
User-written code that executes whenever a given DBMS event occurs, often initiating one or more additional activities outside the DBMS. For example, a given change to a table might cause an email message to be generated or an alarm to beep. Event alerters are similar to **triggers**. They help make the DBMS environment more "active," enabling site-specific business policies to be enforced automatically.

File link
A mechanism that enables external data (usually in file systems) to be managed by a universal DBMS in various ways. The DBMS can be instructed to provide for integrity, security, and recovery of external data referenced by a file link.

Hierarchy
See **class hierarchy, table hierarchy,** and **type hierarchy**.

Impedance mismatch
Fundamental differences in object-oriented programming mechanisms and relational DBMSs that make it difficult to bridge the gap

between these two technologies. These differences involve the range of supported data types and data structures, as well as the typical approach to data access.

Index
A DBMS structure similar in concept to the index of a book. For many operations, indexes can speed access to requested data.

Inheritance
An object-oriented programming mechanism that enables subclasses to automatically inherit or acquire the characteristics and functions associated with their parent class(es).

Instance
An object that belongs to a specific class. For example, "95141" is an instance of US_ZIPCODE.

Instantiable
In a universal DBMS, a user-defined data type that enables firms to create instances of it. If COMPANY were defined as an instantiable data type, specific instances of companies could be created, such as "IBM," "Oracle," or "Microsoft."

Join
A relational algebraic operation that enables users to bring together rows (usually from different tables) based on the truth of some condition. Joins are highly useful, but often expensive, operations to perform.

Large object
A data type supported by a number of relational DBMSs and universal DBMSs. Large objects may contain up to 2 GB or more of data. They contain no internal structure known to the DBMS. A

BLOB is a form of large object used for storing binary data. A CLOB is a form of large object used for storing character data.

List
A type of **collection.** An ordered group of data values. New values are appended to the end of the list. Accessing a given element of the list requires starting at the beginning. Lists have no predefined length or boundary. See also **array, bag, set.**

Method
Sometimes called member function. In object-oriented programming, methods provide services for objects or define the valid "behaviors" (functions) of objects.

Mutator
A function used for changing data within a complex data type.

Object
Software entities that consist of data and code. A number of programming languages allow for the creation of objects, such as Java, C++, and Smalltalk. Class definitions specify the attributes or characteristics of the data as well as the code (functions) that can be applied to an object. An object is said to be an **instance** of its class.

Object/relational
A technology that seeks to integrate many object-oriented and relational concepts. Exactly what constitutes an "object/relational" system is subject to debate. However, the term is often used interchangeably with "universal DBMS" to refer to a system based on the relational approach that has been extended to support such features as user-defined types (both simple and complex), user-defined functions, "unusual" or denormalized table structures, type hierarchies, and others. Note that some extensions may constitute deviations from the relational data model.

Observer
A function used for retrieving or reading data contained within a complex data type.

Optimizer
The component of a relational or universal DBMS that determines an efficient data access strategy for satisfying a query.

Overloading
In a universal DBMS, the ability to enable multiple functions to share the same name or multiple operations to share the same operator (or symbol). For example, many tax functions could be defined to compute the tax rates for different types of entities (clothing, liquor, food, etc.). Each tax function, although different, could bear the "TAX" name. Expected input parameters would be of different data types, enabling the DBMS to correctly determine which TAX routine to execute.

Persistence
The ability to make an object persist, or continue to exist, after the application that created it has completed execution. DBMSs are usually employed to achieve persistence. Object DBMSs, in particular, have focused on providing smooth, integrated support for persistence.

Reference
A data type supported by some universal DBMSs that facilitates navigational-style access and is used in some database designs to explicitly represent data relationships.

Referential integrity
An integrity rule that is part of the relational data model. A DBMS that provides for referential integrity enables administrators to de-

clare that data values of one or more columns in a table must be a subset of the values of one or more other columns in the same or different tables. For example, a firm might require that the department numbers stored in the EMPLOYEE table must correspond to a department number stored in the DEPT table. This prevents employees from being assigned to "invalid" or nonexistent departments.

Relational

A data model employed (to varying degrees) by many popular commercial offerings. Users of relational DBMSs perceive their data to be stored in simple tables. A high-level, set-oriented database access language enables users to work with the DBMS without having to navigate through data structures or provide a specific data access path. Commercial offerings use **SQL** as their standard language.

Row type

A specific form of a complex, user-defined data type. Row types are typically used for table definitions.

Set

A type of **collection.** An unordered group of data values that does not contain duplicates. See also **array, bag, list.**

Simple data type

A data type that contains no internal structure.

SQL

Structured Query Language, the standard interface to relational DBMSs.

SQL3

Nickname for the new SQL specification under development by the International Organization for Standardization (ISO) as of this writing.

Stored procedures
User-written code that helps minimize network traffic in client/server and multitier environments. Stored procedures reside on the same system as the DBMS, typically contain multiple SQL statements, and may be used by multiple applications to perform routine DBMS queries.

Strong typing
A mechanism supported by some object-oriented programming languages and universal DBMSs to provide for greater levels of integrity. Strong typing helps ensure that certain nonsensical operations don't occur, such as directly comparing a value of one data type with the value of a different data type.

Subtype
A user-defined data type derived from one or more other data types. For example, an EXECUTIVE data type might be defined as a subtype of an EMPLOYEE data type.

Table hierarchy
A database design option wherein the structure of new tables is derived from existing tables. A subtable inherits the characteristics of its parent or supertable and typically features additional columns not found in the parent. Queries involving the parent table automatically involve data associated with its subtable(s).

Trigger
User-written code that executes whenever a given DBMS event occurs, often initiating one or more additional DBMS events. Triggers help make the DBMS environment more "active," enabling site-specific business policies to be enforced automatically. Triggers are similar to **event alerters,** but trigger actions may result in other DBMS activities, not external activities.

Type hierarchy

Similar to a **class hierarchy**. In a universal DBMS, user-defined data types can be derived from previously defined data types. **Subtypes** are considered "beneath" their parent type(s) in the type hierarchy.

Universal DBMS

A DBMS said to be capable of supporting the "universe" of data types and a wide range of applications. This term is rather vague and is often used as a catch-all term to describe a considerable range of fundamentally different offerings. In this book, a universal DBMS is defined to be one that attempts to blend object-oriented and relational technologies in a single, highly integrated environment. Extensibility is a key feature.

References and Related Readings

By now you've learned what universal DBMSs are like and what value they can bring to the IT community. If you want to learn more about some of the topics discussed in this book, consider the sources mentioned in this section.

Commercial Activities

Commercial implementations of object/relational technology vary considerably. The following publications describe products that support object/relational capabilities in various forms. Some discuss universal DBMSs, as the term has been defined in this text.

- Bontempo, Charles J., and Cindy M. Saracco. "Supporting Objects in a DBMS." *InfoDB,* Vol. 7, No. 2, Spring 1993.
- Chamberlin, Don. *Using the New DB2: IBM's Object-Relational Database System.* San Francisco: Morgan Kaufmann, 1996.
- Davis, Judith. *DataLinks: Managing External Data with DB2 Universal Database.* InfoIT report, August 1997.
- Davis, Judith. *Oracle8: The Object-Relational Evolution.* InfoIT report, June 1997.
- Davis, Judith. "Universal Servers, Parts I and II." *DBMS,* Vol. 10, No. 7, June 1997 and Vol. 10, No. 8, July 1997.
- Kim, Won. "UniSQL/X: A Unified Database System." *AIXpert,* May 1993.
- *Next-Generation Software Solutions.* UniSQL, SBR-CO-0392, 1992.
- Saracco, Cindy M., and Charles J. Bontempo. "Applying Object Concepts to the DB2 Family." *IDUG Journal,* Vol. 2, No. 1, January 1995.

- Stonebraker, Michael, and Dorothy Moore. *Object-Relational DBMSs: The Next Great Wave.* San Francisco: Morgan Kaufmann, 1996.

- Varma, S. *Uncertain Universality: Coming Soon Through a Vendor near You.* Gartner Group Strategic Analysis Report, September 23, 1997, R-450-107.

- Vermeulen, Robert. "Pushing the Limits." *Object Magazine,* August 1997.

- Wells, David, and Mark Stevenson. *Ovum Evaluates Object/Relational Databases.* Ovum Ltd., UK, 1997.

Research Activities

Universal DBMSs drew heavily on academic and commercial research efforts. Much work continues to be published in research areas, both on theoretical issues as well as lessons learned from prototypes. A good starting point for understanding various research activities is to review the following publications.

- Cheng, J. M., N. M. Mattos, D. D. Chamberlin, and L. G. DiMichiel. "Extending Database Technology for New Applications." *IBM Systems Journal,* Vol. 33, No. 2, 1994.

- Codd, E. F. "Extending the Relational Database Model to Capture More Meaning." *ACM Transactions on Database Systems,* Vol. 4, No. 4, December 1979.

- Codd, E. F. *The Relational Model for Database Management Version 2.* Reading, MA: Addison-Wesley, 1990.

- Darwen, Hugh, and C. J. Date. "The Third Manifesto." *SIGMOD Record,* Vol. 24, No. 1, March 1995.

- Lohman, Guy M., Bruce Lindsay, Hamid Pirahesh, and K. Bernard Schiefer. "Extensions to Starburst: Objects, Types, Functions, and Rules." *Communications of the ACM,* Vol. 34, No. 10, October 1991.

- Stonebraker, Michael. "Inclusion of New Types in Relational Data Base Systems." In *Readings in Database Systems,* Michael Stonebraker, ed., San Francisco: Morgan Kaufmann, 1995.

- Stonebraker, Michael, and Greg Kemnitz. "The POSTGRES Next-Generation Database Management System." *Communications of the ACM,* Vol. 34, No. 11, October 1991.

- *Third-Generation Data Base System Manifesto.* The Committee for Advanced DBMS Function, U.C. Berkeley, Memorandum No. UCB/ERL M90/28, April 9, 1990.

General DBMS

Like the relational DBMSs upon which they were based, universal DBMSs must provide for effective management of shared data. Therefore, working with a universal DBMS presumes a fundamental knowledge of database management in general and relational DBMS technology in particular. The following publications are good sources of material on these subjects.

- Bontempo, Charles J., and Cynthia Maro Saracco. *Database Management Principles and Products.* Englewood Cliffs, NJ: Prentice Hall, 1995.

- Codd, E. F. "A Relational Model of Data for Large Shared Data Banks." *Communications of the ACM,* Vol. 13, No. 6, 1970.

- Codd, E. F. *The Relational Model for Database Management Version 2.* Reading, MA: Addison-Wesley, 1990.

- Date, C. J. *An Introduction to Database Systems, Volume 1,* sixth edition. Reading, MA: Addison-Wesley, 1994.

- Date, C. J. *An Introduction to Database Systems, Volume 2,* Reading, MA: Addison-Wesley, 1982.

- Date, C. J., and Hugh Darwen. *A Guide to the SQL Standard.* Reading, MA: Addison-Wesley, 1997.

- Gray, Jim, and Andreas Reuter. *Transaction Processing: Concepts and Techniques.* San Francisco: Morgan Kaufmann, 1993.

- Selinger, P. G., M. M. Astrahan, D. D. Chamberlin, R. A. Lorie, and T. G. Price. *Access Path Selection in a Relational Database Management System.* IBM Research Report RJ-2429, January 1979.

- Stonebraker, Michael, ed. *The Ingres Papers: Anatomy of a Relational Database System.* Reading, MA: Addison-Wesley, 1986.

- Stonebraker, Michael, ed. *Readings in Database Systems.* San Francisco: Morgan Kaufmann, 1995.

Object Technology

As you've seen, universal DBMSs draw heavily on a number of object-oriented concepts. The following publications describe these concepts, as well as discuss object DBMS systems and component-based architectures (potentially alternatives to universal DBMSs).

- Atkinson, Malcolm, Francois Bancilhon, David DeWitt, Klaus Dittrich, David Maier, and Stanley Zdonik. "The Object-Oriented Database System Manifesto." *Proceedings of the First International Conference on Deductive and Object-Oriented Databases.* Kyoto, Japan, July 1989.

- Barry, Douglas K. *The Object Database Handbook: How to Select, Implement, and Use Object-Oriented Databases.* New York: John Wiley and Sons, 1996.

- Butterworth, Paul, Allen Otis, and Jacob Stein. "The Gemstone Object Database Management System." *Communications of the ACM,* Vol. 34, No. 10, October 1991.

- Cattell, R. G. G. *Object Data Management.* Reading, MA: Addison-Wesley, 1994.

- Cattell, R. G. G., and Douglas K. Barry, eds. *The Object Database Standard: ODMG 2.0.* San Francisco: Morgan Kaufmann, 1997.

- Deux, O., et al. "The O_2 System." *Communications of the ACM,* Vol. 34, No. 10, October 1991.

- Goodman, Nathan. "The Object Data Model." *InfoDB,* Vol. 6, No. 1, Spring/Summer 1991.

- Kim, Won. *Introduction to Object-Oriented Databases.* Cambridge, MA: MIT Press, 1990.

- Lamb, Charles, Gordon Landis, Jack Orenstein, and Dan Weinreb. "The ObjectStore Database System." *Communications of the ACM,* Vol. 34, No. 10, October 1991.

- Loomis, Mary E. S. *Object Databases: The Essentials.* Reading, MA: Addison-Wesley, 1994.

- Raunch, Stephen. "Manage Data from Myriad Sources with the Universal Data Access Interfaces." *Microsoft Systems Journal,* No. 9, Vol. 12, Sept. 1997.

- Saracco, Cindy M. "Writing an Object DBMS Application: Parts 1 and 2." *InfoDB,* Vol. 7, No. 4, Winter 1993/1994 and Vol. 8, No. 1, Spring 1994.

- Taylor, David A. *Object-Oriented Technology: A Manager's Guide,* second edition. Reading, MA: Addison-Wesley, 1997.

Web-Accessible Resources

Finally, a variety of relevant material is accessible via the World Wide Web. Here's a sampling of useful URLs that were valid at press time.

Vendor Activities. Many vendors are active in the universal DBMS arena or offer an alternative to the technology described here. In alphabetical order, some of the major vendors include

- Computer Associates: *http://www.cai.com*
- GemStone Systems: *http://www.gemstone.com*
- IBEX Object Systems: *http://www.iprolink.ch/ibexcom*
- IBM: *http://www.software.ibm.com/data*
- Informix: *http://www.informix.com*
- Microsoft: *http://www.microsoft.com*
- Object Design, Inc: *http://www.odi.com*
- Objectivity: *http://www.objectivity.com*
- Ontos: *http://www.ontos.com*
- Oracle: *http://www.oracle.com*
- O_2 Technology: *http://www.o2tech.com*
- Persistence Software: *http://www.persistence.com*
- Poet: *http://www.poet.com*
- Rogue Wave Software: *http://www.roguewave.com*
- Sun Microsystems: *http://www.javasoft.com*
- Sybase: *http://www.sybase.com*
- Tandem (a Compaq company): *http://www.tandem.com*
- Teradata (NCR): *http://www.teradata.com*
- UniSQL: *http://www.unisql.com*
- Versant: *http://www.versant.com*

References and Related Readings

Magazines and Trade Journals. A number of magazines and trade journals focus largely on DBMS technology and/or object-oriented technology. In alphabetical order, a sampling of these magazines that maintain Web sites include

- *Database Programming and Design: http://www.dbpd.com*
- *Data Management Review: http://www.dmreview.com*
- *DBMS Magazine: http://www.dbmsmag.com*
- *DB2 Magazine: http://www.db2mag.com*
- *Informix Cyber Planet: http://www.informix.com* (follow links to news room/library)
- *Object Magazine: http://www.sigs.com/omo/*
- *Oracle Magazine: http://www.oramag.com*
- *Teradata Review: http://www.teradatareview.com*
- *The Data Administration Newsletter (TDAN): http://www.tdan.com*

Standardization Efforts. Standarization efforts are underway that affect both object/relational (or universal) DBMSs as well as object DBMSs. These sites provide additional information:

- ISO SQL Standard activities: *http://ftp.digital.com/pub/standards/sql* and *ftp://jerry.ece.umassd.edu/isowg3*
- Object Database Management Group (ODMG) activities: *http://www.odmg.org*

Index

A

abstract classes, 111–112
abstract data types (ADTs), 56, 239
activities for triggers, 81
addresses
    complex data types for, 57–59
    subtyping data types for, 107–109
address space for user-defined functions, 93–94
adjustment factors in optimization, 153
administration issues
    in specialized servers with integration layer, 210
    in user-defined functions, 93–94
ADTs (abstract data types), 56, 239
alternative DBMSs, 199–200
    component-based software, 211–213
    object, 201–205
    object/relational mapping services, 205–208
    specialized servers with integration layer, 208–210
analyses
    new forms of, 218
    push-down, 195
    for specialized data, 13
    for temporal data, 166
AND logic for CHECK constraints, 79–80
animation in Web pages, 14
ANSI/ISO interfaces, 188
APIs (application programming interfaces) for multidatabase servers, 184, 193
application development tools, 230
arguments in function overloading, 97
arrays, 120, 239
artwork, libraries for, 168–170
attributes in object-oriented programming, 6
audio data, 12. *See also* large objects
    libraries for, 172
    in Web pages, 14
automatic business rule enforcement
    CHECK constraints for, 78–88
    triggers for, 80–88
AVI format, 171

B

B+-tree indexes, 33, 134–136
    defined, 239
    enhanced, 148
    extending, 142–145
backup operations
    with external indexes, 141
    with file links, 179, 182
bags, 120, 239
bandwidth for large objects, 43–44
behaviors
    in user-defined data types, 48
    in user-defined functions, 29, 94–95
benchmark data, 229
bitmap indexes, 136
BLOBs (binary large objects), 40, 244
blocked files, 179–180
blueprints for complex data types, 111–112
BMP format, 170

Boolean comparisons, 79–80
broken pointers, 179
brokerage firms, libraries for, 163
buffers for large objects, 44–45
built-in functions, limitations of, 28–29
business rules, 25, 77
    automatic enforcement of, 78–80
    benefits of, 29–30
    CHECK constraints for, 79–80
    for external events, 88–90
    guidelines for, 227–228
    stored procedures for, 27–28
    triggers for, 25–26, 80–88
    user-defined functions for, 28–29

C

C++ language, 6
calendars in time series data, 164–166
call-level interfaces, 184
capacity planning, 235
cascading trigger actions, 82
casting, 51–52, 239
catalogs
    defined, 240
    multidatabase servers for, 189–195
    for optimization, 150, 154
    for user-defined data types, 48
chain reactions from triggers, 82
character large objects (CLOBs), 40, 244
CHECK constraints, 79–80
classes
    defined, 240
    inheritance in, 106
    in object-oriented programming, 6, 8
class hierarchies
    defined, 240
    in object-oriented programming, 8–10
class libraries, 36–37
    audio, 172
    benefits of, 157–158
    building, 159
    data cleansing, 172
    defined, 240
    guidelines for, 230–231
    image data, 168–170
    indexes with, 137
    limitations of, 159–160
    spatial, 160–163
    standards for, 172
    text data, 166–168
    time series, 163–166
    video data, 170–171
    Web, 171
client-centric architecture, 204
clients, network calls by, 99–100
client/server architecture, 188
CLOBs (character large objects), 40, 244
clothing industry, specialized data in, 11
CODASYL DBMSs, 2–3
code
    in object-oriented programming, 6
    in relational DBMSs, 8
code reuse, 218
    in object-oriented programming, 5
    stored procedures for, 28, 98–102
    user-defined functions for, 29
coding requirements in vendor offerings, 226–228
collections, 119–120
    combined with complex types and hierarchies, 126–128
    defined, 240
    for multivalue columns, 120–124
    for nested table structures, 124–126

columns, complex data types for, 56–65
commercial activities, reference materials for, 249–250
commit operations
　with file links, 180
　with large objects, 46
commodities, libraries for, 163
comparisons
　with constraints, 79–80
　of large objects, 42
　with strong typing, 51
compatibility of revolutionary DBMSs, 16
complementary tools
　for evolutionary DBMSs, 17
　guidelines for, 230–231
　for revolutionary DBMSs, 16
complex data types, 55–56
　blueprints for, 111–112
　changing data in, 64–65
　for columns, 56–65
　combined with collections and hierarchies, 126–128
　constructor functions for, 60–61
　defined, 241
　hierarchies of, 112–114
　inserting rows in, 61–62
　mutator functions for, 61, 64–65
　observer functions for, 61–63
　references to, 68–73
　retrieving data from, 62–63
　rows with, 31–32
　substituting, 110–111
　subtyping, 107–109
　for table structures, 65–68
　in vendor offerings, 226
complex user-defined functions, 92–93

component-based software, 211–213
compression for image libraries, 170
computer-aided design applications, 201
conditional logic statements, 27
connectivity issues, 235
constraints
　for business rules, 79–80
　calendar systems for, 165
　defined, 241
constructor functions, 60–61, 241
containers. *See* collections
containment information in spatial data, 162
content-based image searches, 170
corporate data vs. specialized data, 10–13
cost estimation in optimization, 153–154
currency data, 12
custom data, 12
custom indexes, 34

D

dangling references, 71
data access middleware. *See* multidatabase servers
database gateways, 187
database management systems (DBMSs), 1
　alternative. *See* alternative DBMSs
　defined, 241
　evolution of, 1–4
　object, 201–205
　reference materials for, 251–252
DataBlades libraries, 158
data cleansing libraries, 172
data definition language (DDL), 23
data independence, 3
data integrity. *See* integrity
DataJoiner, 190–192

DataLinker software layer, 183
data modeling. *See* modeling data
data propagation, 186
data source interfaces for multidatabase servers, 196
data transformation, 186–187
data types, 39, 105
    casting of, 51–52, 239
    complex. *See* complex data types
    creating, 23–24
    in function overloading, 97
    hierarchies of, 112–119, 247
    indexes for, 34
    integrated support for, 218
    for large objects, 40–47
    limitations of, 22–23
    managing, 128–129
    for multidatabase servers, 191
    in object DBMSs, 202
    in object-oriented programming, 6–8
    refining and extending, 106–107
    simple, 47–52, 246
    in vendor offerings, 226
data warehousing, 164, 186–187
DBMS catalogs, 48
DB2 database
    file links in, 178, 183
    index extensions in, 144
DB2 Extenders, 158
DDL (data definition language), 23
delete operations
    with file links, 181
    with large objects, 41
    with table hierarchies, 117
denormalized tables, 241
deployment issues, 233
    environmental, 234–235

    staffing, 234
    target applications, 235–236
descriptors to large objects, 41
distance functions, 162
DISTINCT clause, 195
distinct types
    creating, 47–52
    defined, 242
distributed data, 175
    files links for, 175–183
    multidatabase servers for, 183–196
documents. *See* large objects
dot notation, 63–64
drivers for multidatabase servers, 196
duplicate data
    in collections, 120, 122, 125
    DBMSs for, 1

E

encapsulation
    with complex data types, 60, 68
    defined, 242
    in object-oriented programming, 7
    observer functions for, 62
engines for multidatabase servers, 193
environmental issues, 234–235
event alerters, 88–90
    defined, 242
    with external indexes, 141
    in vendor offerings, 228
events for triggers, 81
evolutionary approach to relational DBMSs, 16–18
expense account trigger example, 82–85
extending
    data types, 106–107
    indexes, 142–145

extensibility
　of component-based software, 211
　of specialized servers with integration layer, 210
extensible type systems, 39
external data
　files links for, 175–183
　multidatabase servers for, 183–196
external events, 88–90
external indexes, 138–141

F

federated database management systems. *See* multidatabase servers
file formats
　for image libraries, 170
　for video libraries, 171
file links, 175–176
　benefits of, 176–177
　capabilities of, 178–182
　defined, 242
　sample architecture, 182–183
file references for large objects, 45
filters
　with external indexes, 140
　with multidatabase servers, 195
FINAL keyword, 108–109
flexibility in object-oriented programming, 5–6
flexible structures, tables with, 30–33
foreign keys, referential integrity with, 72–73
formats
　for image libraries, 170
　for video libraries, 171
forward recovery processing, 47
full-text documents, libraries for, 166–168

functional compensation, 186, 189–190
functions
　indexes for, 35
　overloading, 97–98
　user-defined. *See* user-defined functions
future trends, 221–223
fuzzy matching, 168

G

gateways, 187
geographic data, 12
　indexes for, 143–144
　libraries for, 160–163
Geographic Information System (GIS), 13, 143–144
GIF format, 170
global optimization, 189, 194
granularity
　of spatial data, 161
　of triggers, 81
graphics in Web pages, 14
GRIDENTRY data type, 144
grid file indexes, 143–144, 163
guidelines, 225
　business rules, 227–228
　complementary tools and class libraries, 230–231
　data types, 226–227
　integration, 232
　performance, 229–230
　standards compliance and openness, 231
　vendors, 233

H

hash access, 136
hierarchic DBMSs, 2

hierarchies
  combined with complex types and collections, 126–128
  of complex data types, 112–114
  defined, 242
  in object-oriented programming, 8–10
  table. *See* table hierarchies
  in vendor offerings, 227
hints, optimization, 151–152
historical data, libraries for, 164
host variables for large objects, 44
HTML (Hypertext Markup Language), 14
hub servers. *See* multidatabase servers

I

IDMS (Integrated Database Management System), 2–3
image data, 12. *See also* large objects
  libraries for, 168–170
  in Web pages, 14
impedance mismatches, 10, 219, 242–243
importing data, guidelines for, 232
IMS (Information Management System), 2
indexes, 33, 134
  defined, 243
  extending, 142–145
  external, 138–141
  guidelines for, 230
  for large objects, 42
  for new data types, 34
  new structures for, 145–147
  in optimization, 150
  in relational DBMSs, 134–136
  for spatial data, 163
  for table hierarchies, 119
  for text libraries, 168
  for user-defined data types, 137–138
  for user-defined functions, 35, 147–149
infinite loops from triggers, 82
Information Management System (IMS), 2
Informix indexes, 149
inheritance
  defined, 243
  multiple, 109
  in object-oriented programming, 9–10, 106
  in universal DBMSs, 106, 109
  in user-defined data types, 23
  in vendor offerings, 227
input parameters for stored procedures, 27
insert operations
  with complex data types, 61–62
  with file links, 181
  with large objects, 41
  with table hierarchies, 118
instances, 59, 112
  constructor functions for, 60–61
  defined, 243
instantiable data types, 59, 316
INSTANTIABLE keyword, 59
instructions, optimization, 151–152
Integrated Database Management System (IDMS), 2–3
integration, guidelines for, 232, 235
integration layers, specialized servers with, 208–210
integrity
  calendar systems for, 165–166
  improvements in, 218
  for multidatabase servers, 191
  referential. *See* referential integrity
  of user-defined data types, 50–51

interfaces
    call level, 184
    class library, 159
    multidatabase server, 196
I/O processing
    B+-tree indexes for, 136
    for large objects, 43–44

J

Java applets
    libraries for, 36
    in Web pages, 14
Java language, 6
joins
    defined, 243
    for multivalue columns, 121
    for table data, 30
JPEG format, 170

K

key values
    in B+-tree indexes, 134–135
    indexes for, 33
    large objects as, 42
    referential integrity with, 72–73
keyword searches, 167

L

large objects, 40
    defined, 243–244
    guidelines for, 230
    log activities for, 45–47
    memory for, 45
    network bandwidth for, 43–44
    performance of, 43–45
    storing, 41

user-defined functions for, 96–97
    working with, 41–42
leaf pages, 135–136
leverage
    business rules for, 30
    in evolutionary approach to relational
        DBMSs, 17
    libraries for, 36–37, 158
    problems in, 221
    in vendor offerings, 226
libraries. *See* class libraries
line data, 12, 16
links
    to external events, 88–90
    to files. *See* file links
lists, 120, 244
local storage, multidatabase servers for, 189
locators for large objects, 44
locking with network calls, 99
log activities for large objects, 45–47
logic statements in stored procedures, 27

M

magazines, 255
mailing addresses, 57–59
manuals, libraries for, 167
manufacturing, libraries for, 163
mapping services, object/relational, 205–208
mapping types in object-oriented
    programming, 8
marketing collateral, libraries for, 167
MBRs (minimum bounding rectangles),
    144–145, 161
measurements of success, 236
member functions, 317
memory for large objects, 45

memos, libraries for, 167
messages in object-oriented programming, 7
metadata, 240
methods, 6–7, 244
migrating data, evaluation guidelines for, 232
minimum bounding rectangles (MBRs), 144–145, 161
m:n relationships, 126
modeling data, 105–107
    blueprints for, 111–112
    collections for, 119–126
    combining techniques in, 126–128
    hierarchies in, 112–119
    substituting types in, 110–111
    subtyping in, 107–109
    type creation in, 128–129
m:1 relationships, 70, 125
monitoring performance, 230
MPEG-1 format, 171
multidatabase servers, 183–185
    benefits of, 185–187
    capabilities of, 187–192
    sample architecture, 192–196
multidimensional data, indexes for, 163
multimedia data, 12. *See also* large objects
multiple inheritance, 109
multiple triggers, 82
multitier architecture, multidatabase servers for, 188
multivalue data
    collections for, 120–124
    rows with, 30–31
mutator functions, 61, 64–65, 244

N

names in function overloading, 97
natural language in text searches, 168

negators, optimizing, 154
nesting
    table structures, 124–126
    triggers, 82
networked environments, 2–3
    for large objects, 43–44
    multidatabase servers for, 188
    performance in, 99–100
networking, 234
next-generation gateways. *See* multidatabase servers
NOT FINAL keyword, 59, 108
NOT INSTANTIABLE keyword, 112

O

object DBMSs, 201–205
object identifiers (OIDs), 68
object-oriented (OO) programming, 5–10, 201
    synergy with, 219
    trends in, 222
object/relational technology, 18
    defined, 244
    mapping services, 205–208
    reference materials for, 252–253
objects
    defined, 244
    large. *See* large objects
    in object-oriented programming, 6
observer functions, 61–63, 245
ODBC (Open Database Connectivity), 184, 188, 193
OIDs (object identifiers), 68
OLAP (online analytical processing), 136
one-dimensional data, 143
online analytical processing (OLAP), 136
Open Database Connectivity (ODBC), 184, 188, 193

openness, guidelines for, 231
operations in user-defined functions, 94–95
optimization and optimizers, 34, 149–151
    cost estimation in, 153–154
    guidelines for, 230
    hints and instructions for, 151–152
    multidatabase servers for, 189, 194–195
    for object/relational mapping services, 207–208
Oracle, optimization hints by, 151
order of trigger execution, 82
OR logic for CHECK constraints, 79–80
overlap in spatial data, 162
overloading functions, 97–98, 245

P

pages in B+-tree indexes, 135–136
parent classes, 9–10, 106
pass-through mechanisms, 188
path expressions, 71
performance, 33, 133–134. *See also* indexes; optimization and optimizers
    guidelines for, 229–230
    of large objects, 43–45
    of multidatabase servers, 196
    of network calls, 99–100
    of object/relational mapping services, 207–208
    of revolutionary DBMSs, 15–16
    of specialized servers with integration layer, 210
    stored procedures for, 100
    trends in, 222
    of user-defined functions, 93–94
permissions for file links, 179
persistence, 245
persistent objects, 203

personnel information, libraries for, 167
photos, libraries for, 168–170
piecewise retrieval of large objects, 43–44
planning guidelines, 235
point data 12, 160
pointers
    in B+-tree indexes, 135
    to file links, 179
    as references, 69
polygon data, 12, 161–162
primary keys
    large objects as, 42
    referential integrity with, 72–73
procedural languages vs. object-oriented, 6
procedures, stored. *See* stored procedures
project management, 12
proximity in text searches, 168
push-down analysis, 195

Q

quad trees, 163
queries. *See also* searches
    for collections, 123–124
    performance of. *See* indexes; optimization and optimizers
    references in, 71–72
    in relational DBMSs, 3
    with table hierarchies, 116–118
query writing tools, guidelines for, 230
Quicktime format, 171

R

range checking, constraints for, 79–80
ranking
    in image library searches, 170
    in text library searches, 168
read/write permissions for file links, 179

real-world data types, 218
recovery operations
    with external indexes, 141
    with file links, 179
recursion, trigger, 82
redundancy in collections, 120, 122, 125
reference materials
    for commercial activities, 249–250
    for DBMSs, 251–252
    magazines and trade journals, 255
    for object technology, 252–253
    for research activities, 250–251
    for standardization, 255
    for vendor activities, 254
    for World Wide Web, 253–255
references
    to complex data types, 68–73
    creating, 68–70
    for data access, 71–72
    defined, 245
    to large objects, 41, 45
    vs. referential integrity, 72–73
referential integrity
    defined, 245–246
    for file links, 179–180
    keys for, 42
    for references, 71
    vs. references, 72–73
refining data types, 106–107
region trees, 163
relational DBMSs
    challenges for, 4–5
    emergence of, 3
    evolutionary approach to, 16–18
    indexes in, 134–136
    and object-oriented programming, 5–10

revolutionary approach to, 15–16
    specialized data in, 10–13
    and World Wide Web, 13–14
relational models, 246
relationships, references for, 69–70
relaxed table structures, 30–33
relevance
    in image searches, 170
    in text searches, 168
replication, 186, 189
report writing tools, 230
research activities, reference materials for, 250–251
restrictions in vendor offerings, 226
results from stored procedures, 27
resumes, libraries for, 167
retailing, libraries for, 163
reuse, code, 218
    in object-oriented programming, 5
    stored procedures for, 28, 98–102
    user-defined functions for, 29
revolutionary approach to relational DBMSs, 15–16
RIDs (row identifiers)
    in B+-tree indexes, 134–135
    indexes for, 33
    vs. references, 71–72
rollback operations
    for file links, 180
    for large objects, 46
roll forward processing
    for file links, 182
    for large objects, 47
root pages, 135–136
row-based triggers, 81
row identifiers (RIDs)
    in B+-tree indexes, 134–135

indexes for, 33
vs. references, 71–72
rows
  with complex data types, 31–32
  inserting, 61–62
  with multivalue data, 30–31
row types, 56, 246
R-trees, 163
rules, business. *See* business rules

S

salary bonuses trigger example, 86–87
scalability, 219
scalar functions, 92
scrubbing data, libraries for, 172
searches. *See also* queries
  in image libraries, 170
  in text libraries, 167–168
  in video libraries, 171
secondary keys, large objects as, 42
security
  DBMSs for, 1
  with file links, 180
  for user-defined functions, 93–94
select operations
  with complex data types, 62–63
  with file links, 181
servers, multidatabase. *See* multidatabase servers
sets, 120, 122–123, 246
SET statements, 64–65
shadowing techniques, 46–47
SHAPE data type, 144
signatures of functions, 97
simple data types
  creating, 47–52
  defined, 246
simple user-defined functions, 92–93

Smalltalk language, 6
sound data, 12. *See also* large objects
  libraries for, 172
  in Web pages, 14
spatial data, 12, 160–163
specialized data in relational DBMSs, 10–13
specialized servers with integration layer, 208–210
speed. *See* indexes; optimization and optimizers
SQL (Structured Query Language)
  adoption of, 4
  for class library interfaces, 159
  for columns with structured data, 60–65
  defined, 246
  for file links, 181
  index extensions in, 144–145
  for large objects, 41–42
  user-defined data types in, 23
SQL extensions, 90–92
  simple vs. complex functions, 92–93
  for stored procedures, 101
SQL3 specification, 39
  defined, 246
  observer functions in, 62
  for references, 72
staffing issues, 234
standards
  for class libraries, 172
  guidelines for, 231
  reference materials for, 255
statement-based triggers, 81
statistical information for optimization, 150, 154
stocks, libraries for, 163, 166
storage
  of image libraries, 170
  of large objects, 41

storage (*continued*)
    multidatabase servers for, 189
    of table hierarchies, 118–119
stored procedures
    benefits of, 99–100
    for business rules, 27–28
    for code reuse, 28, 98–102
    defined, 247
    in vendor offerings, 228
    writing, 101–102
strong typing
    defined, 247
    integrity with, 50–51
    for keys, 73
    type casting in, 52
    in vendor offerings, 227
Structured Query Language. *See* SQL
    (Structured Query Language)
subclasses, 8–10, 106
subqueries, 123–124
substituting complex data types, 110–111
subtables, 115–118
subtypes
    for complex data types, 107–109
    defined, 247
    as substitute types, 110–111
success measurements, 236
superclasses, 106
support, guidelines for, 233
synonym searches, 167
system catalogs for optimization, 150, 154
system integration issues, 235
system management
    of specialized servers with integration layer, 210
    tools for, 230
    trends in, 222

T

table functions, 93
table hierarchies, 112–114
    defined, 247
    example, 115–116
    managing, 114–115
    storing, 118–119
    working with, 116–118
tables
    denormalized, 241
    with flexible structures, 30–33
    with multivalue columns, 120–124
    in object-oriented programming, 8
    in relational DBMSs, 3
table structures
    complex data types for, 65–68
    nested, 124–126
targeting applications, 235–236
technical support, guidelines for, 233
temporal data analysis, 166
text data, 12
    external indexes for, 139–140
    libraries for, 166–168
    in Web pages, 14
three-dimensional data, 143, 163
TIFF format, 170
time of triggers, 81
time series data, 12, 163–166
tools
    for evolutionary DBMSs, 17
    guidelines for, 230–231
    for revolutionary DBMSs, 16
trade journals, 255

training
    investments in, 234
    necessity of, 219–220
    for revolutionary DBMSs, 16
transactions
    with file links, 179–180
    with large objects, 45–47
    with multidatabase servers, 187–188
translation tables for triggers, 81–82
transparent access, multidatabase servers for, 184, 187–188
travel expenses trigger example, 82–85
trends, 221–223
triggers, 80–82
    for business rules, 25–26
    considerations for, 87–88
    defined, 247
    examples, 82–87
    with external indexes, 141
    in vendor offerings, 228
tuning facilities, guidelines for, 230
two-dimensional data, 143, 163
type casting, 51–52, 239
type hierarchies, 112–119, 248
types. *See* data types

U

Uniform Resource Locators (URLs), 178
universal DBMSs
    benefits of, 217–219
    business rules in, 25–30
    class libraries in, 36–37
    criticisms of, 219–221
    customization in, 21
    data types in, 22–24
    defined, 248
    emergence of, 18
    as evolutionary approach, 16–17
    flexible structures with, 30–33
    for performance, 33–35
UNIX platforms, 231
update operations
    for complex data types, 64–65
    with file links, 181
    for large objects, 41
    with multidatabase servers, 187–188
    with table hierarchies, 117
URLs (Uniform Resource Locators), 178
user-defined data types, 23–24
    indexes for, 137–149
    integrity implications of, 50–51
    simple, 47–52
    user-defined functions with, 94–96
user-defined functions, 90–92
    for business rules, 28–29
    function overloading in, 97–98
    indexes for, 35, 147–149
    for large objects, 96–97
    optimization of, 153–154
    performance, security, and administrative issues in, 93–94
    simple vs. complex, 92–93
    with user-defined types, 94–96
    in vendor offerings, 228

V

valid data, constraints for, 79–80
vendors
    comparing, 226–228
    guidelines for, 233
    reference materials for, 254

video data, 12. *See also* large objects
   libraries for, 170–171
   in Web pages, 14
virtual databases, 184–185
virtual warehouses, 187

W–Z
warehouses
   data, 164, 186–187
   virtual, 187
Web pages, 13–14
   libraries for, 168–171
   multidatabase servers for, 189
   reference materials for, 253–255
Windows NT platform, 231
word stem searches, 167
workweeks in time series data, 164
World Wide Web, 13–14
   integration with, 232
   libraries for, 168–171
   multidatabase servers for, 189
   reference materials for, 253–255
write permissions for file links, 179
writing stored procedures, 101–102